LEATHER
as Art and Craft

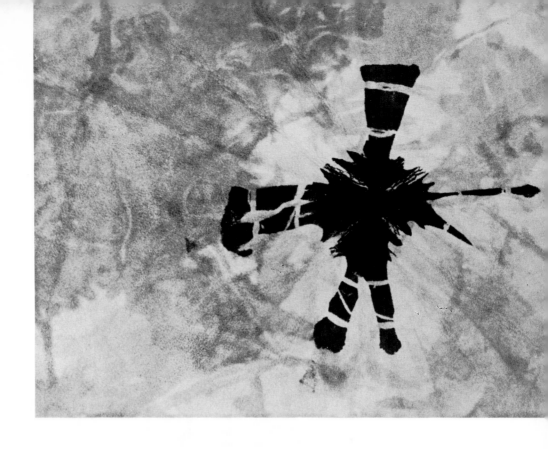

OTHER BOOKS BY THE AUTHOR

Wax as Art Form
Plastics as an Art Form
Plastics as Design Form
Creative Candlemaking
Contemporary Decoupage
Paper as Art and Craft

LEATHER
as Art and Craft

Thelma R. Newman

Crown Publishers, Inc., New York

Inquiries should be addressed to Crown Publishers, Inc., 419 Park Avenue South, New York, N.Y. 10016.

Library of Congress Catalog Card Number: 73–79849

ISBN: 0-517-505746
ISBN: 0-517-505754 pbk

Published simultaneously in Canada by
General Publishing Company Limited

Printed in the United States of America

Design: Nedda Balter

Third Printing, February, 1976

To Jack, Jay, and Lee

Acknowledgments

Leather as Art and Craft owes its existence to a great many people who unselfishly shared their experience and skill with me and and who are credited in the book. Particular thanks goes to Murry Kusmin of Hyannis, Massachusetts, Dan Holiday of St. Augustine, Florida, Ed Viola, John Giordano, Doug Shaffernoth, Jeff Slaboden, and John Elfenbein of New Jersey, Ted St. Germain of Nantucket, Massachusetts, and Walter Dyer of Lynn, Massachusetts. Also Genevieve Barnett of Minneapolis, Mary Fish of Capistrano Beach, California, Yael-Lurie and Jean Pierre Larochette, the Girasol people and Justo Santa Anna Mancera of Mexico, June and John Anderson of New Hope, Pennsylvania. Theirs was a deep involvement from writing about process, taking photos or permitting me to photograph them and their work, and providing in-depth coverage of leather as their art medium.

Much thanks also for special pains in providing photos and descriptions to Dick Muller, Jim and Karen Eagan, Ben Liberty, Fred Williams and his partner A. Dean Massey, Lorne Peterson, Nancy Flanagan, John Fargotstein, and John Cederquist. This list reads like a who's who in leather.

On another front, I received technical help from Foelich Leather Co., Joseph Calistro of A & C Products, Dr. William T. Roddy, director of the Tanners' Research Laboratory of the University of Cincinnati, and Edwin J. Kaine of the New England Tanners' Club.

The following people and groups also gave special service to supply photos, materials, or information: The Tanners' Council of America, Fanny Fibrec of Fibrec, Dr. Frederick Dockstader of the Museum of the American Indian, the Metropolitan Museum of Art, the Museum of Primitive Art, the Museum of Contemporary Crafts, Ed Ghossn of L'Insolite in New York City, and far from last, the excellent Fairtree Gallery in New York.

I have said it before in other books, but it deserves repeating over and over again, that without my husband Jack's constant help in quartermastering and modeling, and assists from my sons Jay and Lee, this book would not have gotten "off the ground."

Special credits, too, to Norm Smith for his "friendly" processing of my photos and for his concern for excellence; and to my friend Madeline McNamara for pitching in when I needed her.

All photographs and diagrams by the author, unless otherwise noted.

CONTENTS

3 "Quartermastery": Tools and Their Uses 36

4 Basic Processes 51

5 Leather Finishing: Exotic Coloring, Tooling, and Burning 113

Preface

"I'm getting out of leather and going into jewelry," exploded a very competent craftsman, after I had admired his work. In what seemed like an endless minute, I recovered to ask him "Why?" "Because," he continued, "it's so limiting. Each leather does its particular thing, and I am getting tired of its sameness and circumscriptions." I am still recovering from that shock. After thinking about what he said from all angles, I've come to the conclusion that the limitations did not belong to leather as a material, but to the craftsman himself. He had gotten into a rut and was smothered by habit.

If *Leather as Art and Craft* has any message for you, it should point out the tremendous potential and diversity possible with leather—even with the restrictions that I have imposed. Namely, that leather always is to look like leather, and not imitate other materials and thereby lose its character and qualities.

Tradition has given us much, but new technology and our broader outlook toward expression today has widely expanded the potential of what leather can do and say. The focus here is contemporary, very much "of and for today." Our book, too, is concept and process oriented. Product usually follows from process. If we understand basic principles, our potential for creativity with leather should stretch.

Leather as Art and Craft can introduce the neophyte to the art and craft of leather, but I hope that it also will prove useful to the experienced leather craftsman by expanding understanding and skill and by providing new information so that one can dip into areas that have not been experienced before.

Leather as Art and Craft should be a complete and self-contained resource because it covers just about every area of expertise, overflows with photographs and diagrams, and provides useful trimmings such as a glossary and a supply source section. For those who wish to explore further, there is also a bibliography.

Some of the greatest talent in the United States and Mexico is represented within. I hope that the illustrations and text will be as inspiring to you as it was exciting for me to research and to write.

LEATHER
as Art and Craft

1

Leather, Then and Now

Leather is an incredible material! It is sensuous and appealing in the way it smells, feels, looks. It excites the senses. When worn as clothing it conforms to the body like another skin. It can be supple, smooth, rigid, rough, solid, spongy, light, heavy, scaly, thick, thin. It can be unpredictable: no two hides, or skins, are the same. It can last for centuries or crumble within years.

Leather can be sewed like fabric; cut, scored, and glued like paper; carved, laminated, and nailed like wood; hammered and tooled like metal; painted like canvas; woven and tied like yarn; formed like papier-mâché; molded like felt; dyed like textiles.

Leather can be the structure itself, or a covering. It can be as insignificant as a bead, or as important as a sculpture. It is both decoration and art; and whether one or the other, ubiquitous leather has communicated in a multitude of ways throughout the ages. It has been so significant as to be the mainstay of a civilization; and as invisible to man as the fifth dimension. Even though leather is one of mankind's earliest known materials, new ways of treating, working, and designing with leather are still being discovered.

LEGENDARY USE OF LEATHER

Tracing the story of leather is like reviewing the history of man. Man's use of leather laces through all civilizations and is transmitted from culture to culture or is developed independently throughout history. Need necessitated invention. That is probably

Egyptian (Coptic) leather head supports to preserve the coiffure date back to the third to seventh century B.C. from Ankmim. *Courtesy The Metropolitan Museum of Art, Gift of George F. Baker, 1890*

why leather is one of the earliest materials used by mankind. Leather certainly was not vital when man had his own ample covering of hair, but as he became less hirsute, he sought covering with clothing and shelter to protect himself from changes in weather. It would be safe to conjecture that as early as Neolithic times man used animal skins for clothing. He domesticated animals, began to settle in villages, made pottery, stone implements, used the bow and arrow, and cultivated grain and fruit trees. He probably even discovered a primitive method of tanning leather. It is quite possible that skins left next to a fire became coated with wood ashes (lye) and with fats from cooking meats. Later he could have smoked them over wood fires finding that this too helped to preserve and soften the skins.

Earliest recorded history dates to cave pictographs (perhaps 20,000 B.C.) showing hunters wearing skins of animals while running after prey. Petroglyphs by Egyptians in tombs dating back to 6000 B.C. depict leather as a tribute to kings and gods.

Indeed, man's customs and vocabulary are also intertwined with this vital material: leather. Leather sandals were important and valued in Egypt. Men of rank are pictured in murals followed by a servant carrying a pair of sandals. Good sandals were expensive, rare, and were not worn except when neces-

sary. Princes appeared before the Pharaoh barefoot; the king alone could wear sandals (but not in the house of his gods). Likewise, the merchant walked barefoot behind the shod prince and so on down the line.

Sandals in Hebrew culture were an important part of the marriage contract. At the end of the ceremony the bride and groom traded sandals as a sign of mutual fidelity. This exchange indicated their intent not to stray from the marital path.

In Greek legend, Zeus, the most mighty of Gods, ruler of the Heavens, is described as wearing the aegis, which originally was a breastplate made of the goat that suckled him. When the breastplate evolved in size, sporting a Gorgon's head, it was associated with Athena. Later on the aegis was the name for a protective leather coat worn by Greek soldiers. To this day "aegis" implies defense, protection, favorable auspices, or leadership.

The goatskin, though, was not the only leather with magical properties. Deerskin beds in the days of the classical Greeks protected the sleeper from snakes. And priests slept on special skins when they wished to invoke oracles in their dreams. In another "world," the Dakota and Cheyenne Indians wore war shirts trimmed with hair; Crow and Blackfeet used weasel skins. These were worn on special occasions by men of authority or by those distinguished in battle, because these special buckskin shirts were considered to hold great medicinal power and protect the wearer from misfortune. (Later the white man called them "scalp shirts," but hair did not always come from enemy scalps.)

Thomas Carlyle in his *Sartor Resartus* theorizes that man who used oxen as money got tired of lugging ox around for barter. Instead, he inscribed a piece of leather with a picture of an ox, hence the Latin word for hide—*pecus.* He put these pieces in his pocket and called it *pecunia.* "Pecuniary" still refers to money. But more than that, slang for the dollar is a "skin." We can "skin" a man in trading. When we succeed (illegally) we are playing a "skin game." And who does not know a skinflint?

We have other sayings that owe their existence to the integrality of leather in our lives. A person who does not get easily perturbed is "thick-skinned" or has a "thick hide." But if he is stubborn, he is "hidebound." Have you ever had your "hide tanned?"

Man's, or rather woman's, ingenuity in face of challenge shows amazing creativity, as is recounted in the story of the founding of Carthage. It was reported that Queen Dido was granted land upon which to build her city, but only as much as could be covered by the hide of a bull. Queen Dido cut the hide into a very thin continuous strip and was able to encircle enough land on which to build her first fort, later the site of Carthage. That would have taken a huge bull, in any case. Do you suppose the story was full of bull?

An African Masai shield from the Kenya-Tanzania area that is not too unlike the early armor of the Romans and Orientals. The leather is exceedingly hard and difficult to penetrate.

Masai women embroidering a leather skin with beads. Leather is worn for special occasions.

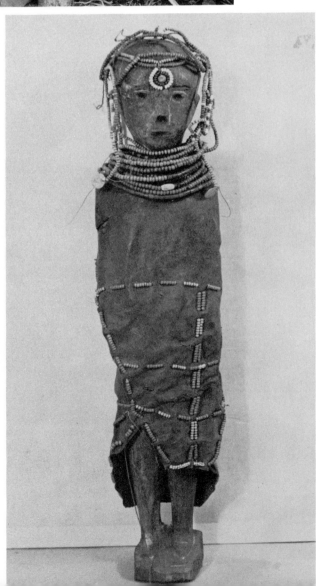

A Masai hand-carved wooden doll adorned with a terra-cotta colored leather "toga." Note the bead embroidery.

THE PATH OF LEATHER AS PROCESS AND PRODUCT

The history of leather, nevertheless, is based on fact and can be traced both by recounting the tanning process and tracing products made of leather. Tanning of leather is a measure of the competency of man and an indicator of man's position in the continuum of human development, for it is the quality of leather and the variety of leathers that lead to a range of products and uses. It served to protect as well as adorn.

Tanning of hides and skins arrests decomposition, increases their strength, makes them more pliable, and keeps them from becoming soluble in water and drying out in air. Indeed, pieces of leather dating back to 1300 B.C. have been found in Egypt. But the tanning of leather much as we know it to this day dates back to the Bronze Age, somewhere around 2500 B.C. Oak tanning, still practiced much the same way to this day, was attributed to the Hebrews. Accordingly, the Hebrews wrote in the Bible, Genesis 3:21, that the first clothing worn by man after his expulsion from the Garden of Eden was made of leather (skins). "Unto Adam and also unto his wife did the Lord God make clothes of skin and clothe them." This reference recording the use of leather dates back six thousand years. The Bible also tells of Moses dyeing rams' skins, and many references are made throughout about girdles (wide belts) and sandals. That tanning was known to be a hard and laborious trade is evidenced in the writings of Rabbi Judah who said: "Happy is he whose art is barbering, and alas for him whose art is tanning."

The only radically different method of tanning, other than oak tanning, was recounted by Homer in the *Iliad*. He describes the chamoising of a skin. The Greeks opened the pores of the hide by repeated washings and oil was forced into the pores by constant heating and rubbing while the hide was stretched on a frame. This soft leather called *shamoy* (predecessor of our modern-day chamois) was used to make much of the Greeks' best clothing. It was a soft beautiful leather, and more than that it was waterproof.

Leather skins and styles, along with much of their culture, were imported from the Greeks by the Romans. Leather tanning

The tradition of style and skill displayed in this leather chess set by an eighteenth-century Spanish leather craftsman dates back to the Moors who brought leather craft from Africa and set up shop in Cordova, Spain. *Courtesy The Metropolitan Museum of Art, Gift of Gustavus A. Pfeiffer, 1948*

was no exception, but they improved on the art. Through variations in their methods of tanning, the Romans made exceptionally soft leather for clothing and exceptionally hard leather for armor. Armor leather was molded to fit the wearer's body while damp from the tanning "pickle." The form was then heat-tempered until it became a rigid armor that was so dense it could deflect arrows or a sword thrust. The Romans also armored their war-horses and chariots with this super-hard leather. But they were not the only leather armor makers. Marco Polo tells of the protective coverings worn by the Tartars of Kublai Khan: "They wear defensive armor made of the thick hide of buffaloes and other beasts, tanned and dried by the fire and thus rendered extremely hard and strong." Today a similar process that introduces pressure as well as heat is used to form armor, gaskets, and coverings for machinery. The material feels as hard as steel, as inflexible, but is comparatively light in weight.

The Babylonians and Assyrians used alum, gallnuts, oil, myrrh, and sumac to produce three varieties of leather. When the Phoenicians invaded North Africa in 1600 B.C., they brought their leather craft to the Moors. The Moors added their own ingenuity and developed a very fine leather that was made from goats. It was called Moroccan goat. These Moroccan hides were used and still are utilized to make the finest bookbindings.

This Fulani, or Maure, saddle-bag from Africa is a predecessor of the Moroccan *Shikara*, a traditional bag carried by men. It is leather appliqué with leather embroidery.

Marco Polo brought back tales of luxurious leather appointments used in the Orient. This Japanese nineteenth-century panel reflects a rich tradition. Its theme is a butter-fly crest stenciled in black on brown leather. *Courtesy The Metropolitan Museum of Art, H. O. Havemeyer Collection*

A Japanese nineteenth-century leather panel was lacquered in colors with the figure of a Tennin. *Courtesy The Metropolitan Museum of Art, H. O. Havemeyer Collection*

When the Moors brought sumac tanning across to Spain in the eighth century, they established their leather arts in Córdova. To this day "Cordovan" is still a fine, well-known leather. The Spanish embroidered their own techniques to leather-decorating traditions that emanated from Ghadames in the Sahara. *Guadamacileros* of Spain excelled in creating figured leather, but always with the figures subordinated to the leather itself.

Although some Near East traditions filtered into Spain by way of the conqueror, Marco Polo spoke of the leather of the Near and Far East. He reported that the Chinese cured skins with mud and salts of alum. Likewise, in Persia medieval tanners were well known for the fine leathers they produced in Gurgan near Mero. (They used goat leather cured with alum and salt, as well as quicklime.) Results were similar to the Moroccan skins.

IMPROVED TANNING OF LEATHER

In most early societies the leather tanning art was a secret passed down from father to son. Secret tradition was preserved that way in Europe and North Africa through tanners' and leatherworkers' guilds. Royal charters or licenses were issued permitting people to practice leather tanning, which further restricted the dissemination of the craft. These guilds, although not in existence in Europe today, are extant in North Africa. The same techniques used by the Moors yesterday have been handed down through the centuries by hereditary guilds, and even their workshops are in the same location in the Fez Medina.

Tanning of leather emerged differently as it evolved through the American Indians. Leather ingenuity and creativeness were important for the Indians of America. Leather was used for wigwams, clothing, moccasins, arrow quivers, and blankets. Tanning was carried out by the squaw. She would flay the animal, removing the skin with a stone or a bone knife, wet it, and stack the skins in piles or bury them until the hair cells loosened. The squaw then soaked the skins in lye solution made from ashes of wood fires, much as the Egyptians had done thousands of years before. Then hides were placed over the trunk

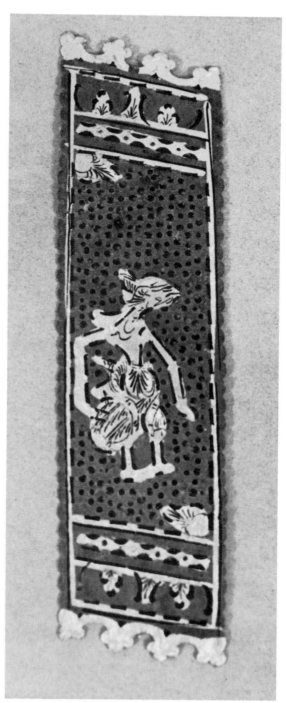

An Indonesian wayang leather bookmark using the same techniques as in the making of shadow puppets. The leather has a perforated pattern similar to their shadow puppets. *Courtesy Brimful House*

Leather mask of Yaqui Indians of the Yuto-Nahua group of Mexico.

Leather has the flexibility and organic qualities that qualify it as another skin—as a mystical face or as ceremonial dress. This mask is an Arizona Hopi Indian "Rain Priest of the North." Combined with leather and paint, fabric, fur, hair, feathers, wood, and cord. *Courtesy The Museum of Primitive Art, New York*

of a tree and scraped with bone tools until both hair and flesh sides were clean. Hides then were dusted with a powder made of wood (her tanning agent contained tannin) and treated with a mixture made from the brain and liver of the animal (her currying compound). This oily mixture was scrubbed into the hides, tanning them with the animal's own natural fluids and components.

Hides then were allowed to set and later were hand-rubbed, crushed, sometimes chewed, until they were soft. The more manipulation, the softer the leather. Smoking the skins in an airtight tepee over a smudge fire for several days, completed the process. The result was buckskin—waterproof, soft, and pliant—the clothing of Indians and later of trappers and explorers as well. Jackets, leg-

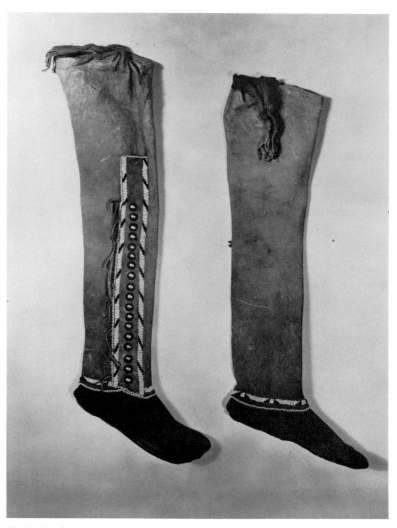

Buckskin legging moccasins of the Shoshoni Indians show the use of beads and buttons as decoration that dates back to earlier traditions of using shell and stone beads as adornment. *Courtesy The Museum of the American Indian, Heye Foundation*

gings, and moccasins often were decorated with porcupine quills, silver, and turquoise, depending upon the tribe. Later trade beads were used. Sometimes berry juices, root extracts, and clays were employed to dye and decorate the buckskin.

When the New World was settled, the newcomers brought with them the tanning process of the Old World and borrowed a few ideas from their Indian neighbors. In 1623 Experience Miller set up the first tannery in Plymouth, Massachusetts. Early tanning vats were out of doors and consisted of a hole dug in the ground walled with heavy planking. Hides were soaked in limewater to loosen hair, then scraped with a knife and placed layer upon layer in vats. Each hide was covered with a sprinkling of fine oak bark (ground with heavy stones). The vat was filled with water and the hides were allowed to remain in the mixture for six months until thoroughly tanned. It is amazing to think that the tanning process made a full circle around the world, met the Indians halfway, and still was very much the same process introduced by the Hebrews many centuries before.

DEVELOPMENT OF MODERN-DAY TANNING

Small changes in the tanning process evolved slowly through the ages. Peter Minuet, governor of New Amsterdam, for instance, invented a horse-drawn stone mill for grinding oak bark. It is startling to think, however, that it was not until the early nineteenth century that any significant scientific study of tanning was made. Sir Humphry Davy, an English scientist, found that other tree barks and some nuts contained tannin. Since hemlock was plentiful in the New World, a new resource was made available. This discovery by Sir Davy led to experiments by chemists who developed chrome-tanned leather. Rather than a vegetable-tanning agent, a mineral, chromium salts, was used. The original results were stiff, but the process took only a few days rather than months, and the light blue-gray color that resulted permitted the use of brilliant and varied colored dyes.

Meanwhile, in 1809, a splitting machine was developed by Samuel Parker of Newburyport, Massachusetts, which made pos-sible the splitting of leather to desired thicknesses. There was no waste; all the leather was used. One workman could split a hundred hides a day instead of four or five with the shaving method. Then in 1850 a Maine tanner named Mellen Bray invented a machine for removing hair and surplus flesh. His machine moved the hide against a series of knives, which were attached to a cylinder that rotated in the opposite direction.

Vegetable tanning still remained the primary tanning method until Robert Foerderer improved on chrome tanning by treating chrome-tanned leather with soap and oil, a process now called "fat liquoring." With this improvement chrome-tanned leather combined the advantages of water resistance and speed of tanning with the durability, workability, and strength found in vegetable-tanned leather. Today 90 percent of all tanning done in the United States, except for tooling leather and leather used in soles of shoes, is chrome-tanned. Chrome tanning shortened the weeks-long process of tanning leather to just days and produced an overall uniformity and a greater variety of purposes.

Today's tanners have three important instruments that further advanced the art of tanning—the thermometer, hydrometer, and an electronic pH meter. The thermometer helps indicate temperature, the hydrometer determines density of solutions, and the electronic pH meter finds alkalinity and acidity of solutions. With modern-day leather splitting and tanning machines, new finishes, new grains, new patterns and properties are possible in leather tanning. All this greatly expands the potential for the use of leather. In 1970 American tanneries processed more than 118 million hides and skins!

HISTORICAL ARRAY OF LEATHER PRODUCTS

Even though the range of leather's potential has been greatly enlarged, the spectrum of products through the ages has always been exceedingly varied and plentiful. For instance, the Eskimos' life depends on skins for fur-lined and hooded parkas, mukluks for their feet, and mittens for their hands. Their tentlike houses are made of skins, and for their transportation kayaks are formed of sealskins stretched over a pointed frame with an opening in the middle where the hunter sits. All skins used for wearing apparel are chewed by Eskimo women to soften them.

Leather has always been associated with man's mobility, as sandals, wheels, and as saddle and harness. Sandals, once deemed precious by the Egyptians, evolved through Hebrew invention until the sandal almost completely covered the wearer's foot, nearly approaching the shape of the modern-day shoe. Sumerians used leather for tires on their chariots and Caesar mentioned the use of leather sails hoisted on ships from Brittany.

The Eskimos weren't the only people who used leather for dwellings. Marco Polo described Kublai Khan's war tents as ". . . made of soft, tanned lion and tiger skins streaked with white, black and red, and so well joined together that neither wind nor rain can penetrate. Within they are lined with ermine and sables which are the most costly of furs." The Marco Polo journals also mentioned the many uses of leather in India and other areas of southern Asia. In referring to Guzerat, a major leatherworking city of India situated on the Indian Ocean, Marco Polo describes: "Coverlets for beds are made of red and blue leather, extremely soft and

Italian leatherwork over wood. The box with its stamped and incised design is circa fifteenth century. *Courtesy The Metropolitan Museum of Art, Rogers Fund, 1950*

Baroque elegance is apparent in the sixteenth-century carved, gilded, and painted case containing toilet accessories from Venice, Italy. *Courtesy The Metropolitan Museum of Art, Rogers Fund, 1927*

Marco Polo's tales and treasures influenced design as did the Moorish conquerors. This French late-fourteenth-century coffret shows an iota of influence with further innovation in incising and embossing leather. *Courtesy The Metropolitan Museum of Art, Gift of Bashford Dean, 1923*

delicate, and stitched with silver and gold thread; upon these the Mahometans are accustomed to repose." These tales were exotic, incredible to Europeans, and if it were not for the fact that Marco Polo brought back examples of Asian art to substantiate his stories, he probably would have been locked up as insane. Fortunately, these pieces influenced product design in Europe instead.

Going back in time to Crete in 1500 B.C., water and grain were stored in leather containers, and leather cups dating back to Neolithic inhabitants of Britain were found near Smithfield, London. And on another continent in another age—American colonial times—leather was used as furniture, door hinges, carriage springs, bottles, and kitchen utensils, as well as clothing and window coverings. In a nondomestic vein, leather became armor to the Romans and Tartars, and was used as a cannon cover (over copper) by the Venetians in 1349. In aboriginal cultures, leather was formed into drums, fetish figures, and shields.

The use of leather reached great heights of artistry during the Middle Ages and in the

On the left is a bottle covered with woven strips of leather and dried palm leaf from Guinea, Africa. The leather is colored burnt sienna. (The cork is not part of the original design.) Leather has been used for centuries as waterproof containers. Next to the bottle is a basket beer pot called an *Ekei*, made by the women of the Abagusii tribe of the Kisii district in Kenya, Africa. These baskets have a skin base with hair left intact; they are used by women for drinking millet beer.

Leather reached heights of artistry particularly as bindings of treasured books. The binding of this A. Coburger (Nuremberg) Bible of the fifteenth century is stamped and incised with metal pieces showing the arms of the Archbishop of Salzburg. *Courtesy The Metropolitan Museum of Art, Fletcher Fund, 1924*

Renaissance when bookbindings of leather were carved, embossed, and inlaid with precious metals and gems and their parchment or vellum pages were illuminated painstakingly with hand lettering and illustration. Parchment and vellum, by the way, are also made of skins. Parchment is fabricated from the split skins of sheep, and vellum is made of calfskin, goatskin, or lambskin exposed for a long time to lime and then scraped with a rounded knife or rubbed smooth with pumice stone. Since neither parchment nor vellum is tanned, they are not, therefore, true leather.

Mask of peccary skin used by the Pharasee, or evil spirit, in a religious dance held just before Easter by the Opata Indians, Opodepe, San Miguel River Valley, Sonora, Mexico. *Courtesy Museum of the American Indian, Heye Foundation*

White fur and leather in a Yaqui Indian mask, Yuto-Nahua group, Mexico.

Another decorating tradition—tooling and embroidering and plaiting of leather— was transmitted by the Moors to Spain and by the Spanish to the New World. Hernando Cortes, in 1520, brought horses to America complete with ornate saddles and complexly braided gear. These skills caught on from Texas all the way to Argentina and still are practiced. But leather decorating was amply evident in pre-Columbian America as well. American Indians embroidered on leather applying porcupine quills (later beads), which were softened in water, flattened, dyed, and then sewn to leather.

This sketchy survey indicates the importance of leather in the daily lives of peoples throughout the ages and suggests the tremendous range of leather's potential. No matter what has been done with leather in the past, and as you can see it was considerable, there are still new variations on process and new design ideas emerging. That's what makes working with leather so exciting!*

* Credits to Dan Holiday for his historical research.

Leather has a universality of use that transcends centuries, yet for each age it expresses very different designs and concepts. "Large Autumn Branch" by Murry Kusmin.

Formed leather paperweight by Ed Viola.

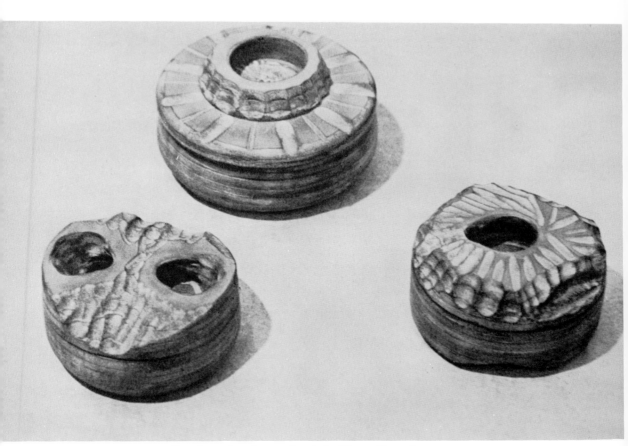

Laminated and carved pots by Murry Kusmin.

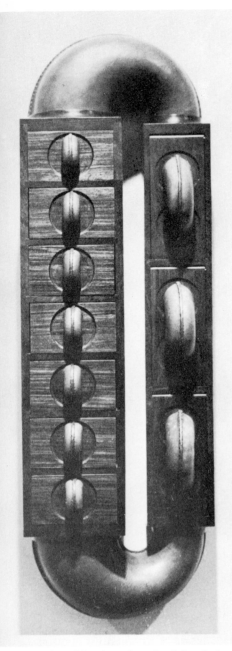

A wood and leather chest by John Cederquist.

Leather-covered "womb chair" by Eero Saarinen.

2

Kinds of Leathers and Their Uses

WHAT IS LEATHER

Leather, a natural phenomenon, consists of an awesome architecture beneath its surface. It is leather's remarkable, natural structure, and the way it has been preserved by the tanner, that to this day serves mankind as it has through the ages.

Leather can be defined in various ways: from a sensory point of view such as how leather looks or feels; from a manufacturing stance as to how leather is prepared and dressed; and from a scientific point of view utilizing a biologist's and chemist's insights. All definitions are valid and necessary in order to completely comprehend the material; all viewpoints should be considered.

FROM A SCIENTIFIC VANTAGE POINT

Every mammal has skin. This skin consists of three layers. The thin outer layer is called the epidermis, which is made of scale-like cells that flake or peel away. The second layer is a thick inner skin called the corium, which is composed of a fine fibrous material, collagen, that gives the skin its elasticity. In the corium there are also sweat glands, hair follicles, sebaceous glands that lubricate the hair, and small blood vessels and nerves. The third layer is made of subcutaneous fatty tissue consisting of bands of connective tissue, globules of fat, larger blood vessels, and more nerves. The fatty layer serves to protect mammals from cold and acts as a reserve supply of food in the living animal, but once the mammal is killed, bacteria spread, causing putrification and eventual decay of the entire skin.

TRADITIONAL PROCESSES

PREPARATION AND CURING OF HIDES

The first stage in preparing a skin was to remove that fatty layer, usually by scraping it away. This had been accomplished in the past with stone tools and later with metal knives. The process is known as *scuding,* or *fleshing.* Some people soaked the hide in water, followed by pounding the hide to accelerate the process. The second preparatory step was to remove the pelt (hair) and epidermis, because what we want to eventually be left with is the corium. Hair was removed, in the past, simply by scraping it away. Some people learned to cut down the labor of scraping the hide by *sweating* the hide, which was placing it in urine that became highly alkaline and hastened the decay of the hair, loosening it so that scraping later on was facilitated. A currier's comb was generally used for this. It is a tool with teeth set in a circle. Some people hastened the decay of the hair by soaking the hide in quicklime and water, or with fresh wood ashes rubbed into the moistened surface. After hair removal, the hide was chemically washed to prevent further chemical attack and to remove other nonleather components in the grain. This is called *bating.*

DRESSING

I dry the skins out in the air
Removing first each clinging hair.
Then in the Escher stream I dash them
And thoroughly from dirt I wash them.
Cow-skin and calf in tan I keep,
Long months in bark-soaked water steep
Then with a brush of hair I scrape them
And on the selling counter drape them.

—Hans Sachs, 1568, Nuremberg
poet-shoemaker known as
"Nightingale of the Reformation"

Once fat and pelt were removed, the hide needed to be treated to prevent further bacterial decay. Hides were preserved or dressed in various ways—by smoking, whereby the hide absorbed resinous materials

Tanned hides are removed from tanning drum. *Courtesy Edwin J. Kaine, New England Tanners' Club*

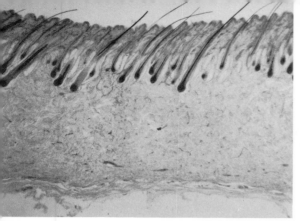

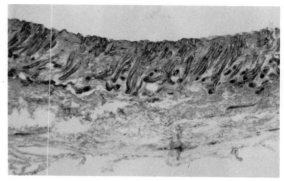

The following cross sections of skins and hides are magnified twelve times. *All photos courtesy Tanners' Council Research Laboratory, University of Cincinnati, Cincinnati, Ohio*
This example is an enlarged cross section of fresh calfskin.

Cross section of fresh wool sheep (Merino).

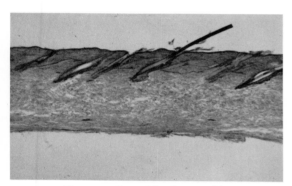

Cross section of fresh goatskin.

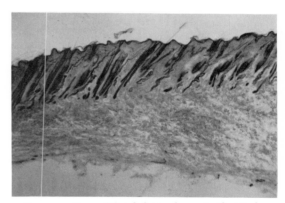

Cross section of fresh hair sheep (cabretta).

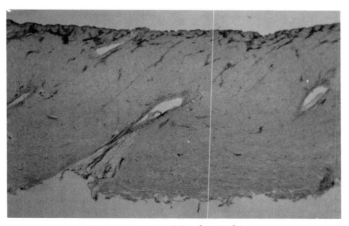

Cross section of fresh pigskin.

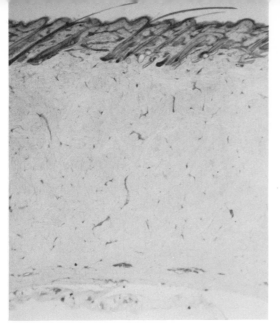

Cross section of fresh steerhide.

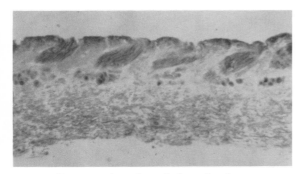

Cross section of wool sheep leather.

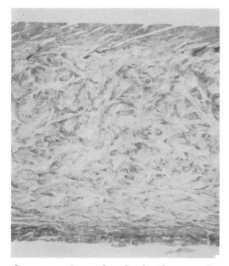

Cross section of sole leather made from steerhide.

BASIC DIFFERENCES OF LEATHERS AND CLASSIFICATION

Even though each skin, or hide, is subjected to the same treatment, leathers have characteristic grains and individual "personalities." Essentially, this is due to different arrangements of hair follicles, sweat glands, and patterns of blood vessels, as well as varying qualities from fine to coarse in the arrangement of the collagen fibers. No two hides are the same even within the same class of mammal.

The appeal or feel of leather results from its natural architecture. This distinctive architecture is created by a tremendous number of fiber bundles, each bundle interlaced with tiny fibers. Each fiber is a spiral, cable-like cord of complex proteins that has been stabilized in tanning. Leather is an intricate matrix made up of millions of fibrils that unite to form fibers. And in turn the fibers form bundles that interlock into a matrix. If these fibers were to be measured, they would add up to about thirty acres of internal surface per pound of leather.* The makeup of the matrix and the pattern of blood vessels, as well as surface hair, give leather its unique grain or pattern.

Classifying hides becomes a problem because of these differences. Generally, though, hides are categorized or should be demarcated by their source, the animal it came from, and by the treatment the hide has undergone. However, this still can be a bit confusing. For example, "kidskin" and "chamois" should imply that one is the skin of kid and the other the skin of chamois, but it really indicates that lambskin has undergone different treatments. "Morocco" should indicate that it came from goatskin, was sumac tanned, and dyed red. "Cordovan" also should indicate that it is horsehide, sumac tanned, and later tanned with an infusion of sumac. Likewise, "Russian leather" should mean that the leather is calfskin, which was dressed with birch oil. But modern leather technology has advanced to the point where *imitations look like the names they take,* making meanings imprecise.

* Courtesy Dr. William T. Roddy, Director, Tanners' Research Laboratory, University of Cincinnati.

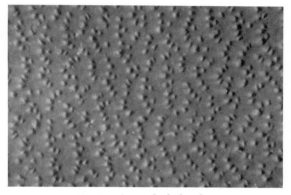

These are enlargements (fifteen times) of different leathers. *All photos courtesy Tanners' Council Research Laboratory, University of Cincinnati, Cincinnati, Ohio*

This particular skin is the grain of calfskin leather. Note the differences in surface appearance made by hair growth patterns.

Grain of steerhide leather.

Grain of horsehide leather.

Grain of deerskin leather.

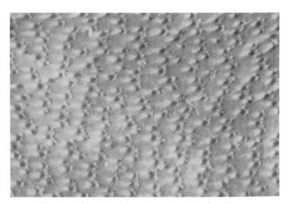

Grain of hair sheep (cabretta) leather.

Grain of pigskin leather.

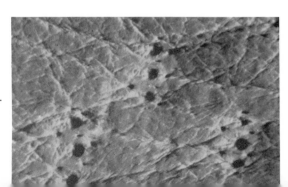

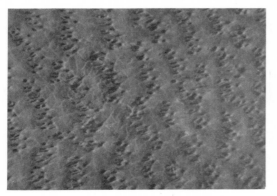

Grain of wool sheep (Merino) leather.

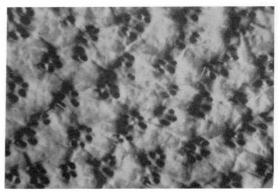

Grain of camel-hide leather.

Surface of suede leather enlarged as the others fifteen times.

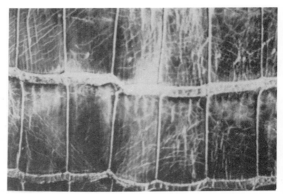

Grain of alligator leather enlarged three times.

Calfskin leather tanned with the hair on the skin. Natural size.

Generally, finer leathers come from smaller animals such as goats, sheep, young deer, or smaller or younger versions of larger animals such as calves rather than cows. Leathers from these small animals have been called "skins." Hides come from large animals such as horses, cows, and buffalo. Thickness of leather is also no measure of quality because coarser leathers can be split to produce several sheets of thin leather. Quality is also related to an animal's environment such as the climate of the land, the type of feed, injuries to the body, etc. Slaughter cuts in the pelt caused by mishandling at meat-packing establishments can also reduce a hide's attributes, and if hides and skins are not cleaned and treated quickly to prevent putrefaction, they begin to decompose and lose the plasticity of the collagen fibers within hours. Some modern-day processes correct this, but do not completely reverse degradation.

PHYSICAL PROPERTIES OF LEATHER

BREATHING AND INSULATING PROPERTIES

Leather can breathe because its densely packed fibrous structure permits a continuous movement of air and water. When wearing leather, if the body perspires, the leather has sufficient porosity to allow moisture on the skin to evaporate.

As insulation the matrix of leather fibers contains millions of tiny voids, or air spaces, that provide protection from wind and a certain amount of cold air.

CAPACITY TO ABSORB AND TRANSMIT MOISTURE

Most leathers are hydrophilic, that is, they possess a certain affinity for moisture. Leather picks up a certain amount of moisture in the air, and it will wick away water from any damp material with which it comes in contact. Some small amount of moisture is good for leather, helping to lubricate the fibers. When water content increases, leather tends to stretch.

Chamois will absorb at least 3½ times its weight of water. Some leathers that have been "stuffed" in tannage will have little water absorption (but will absorb perspiration). The tanner can control properties in

tannage to a certain extent, making leathers for specific end uses.

FLEXIBILITY

The matrix of fibers that makes up leather is a random configuration; therefore, it does not matter which way leather is flexed, whether top to bottom, side to side, grain out or in. Leather can be almost continuously flexed and will return to its original shape unless it dries out from heat caused by flexing. Mineral tannages, such as chrome, produce greater thermal stability than do most organic tannages such as vegetable. In order to maintain a flexed position the leather has to be hammered or tied into that shape.

STRENGTH

The strength of a leather is an important determinant as to its use. Leather when stretched for a test of its tensile strength (test of flexibility) is one of the strongest flexible sheets known to man. The collagen molecules of the corium possess a helical shape much like a coil spring that untwists and returns to its shape when flexed and pulled. Leather, therefore, can be stretched, pulled, and tugged without breaking or tearing. Notice what happens to the leather of your gloves as you pull them on or off—the leather returns to its original form without tearing and losing its original configurations.

Since leathers are not oriented to any fixed directional pattern, there is no oriented path for tearing and there is no easy path for a tear to follow. Because of this, it is not necessary to make a hem or bend over the edge of a piece of leather. On the other hand, a punched hole or slit will stay that way.

ELONGATION

Elongation relates, on the whole, to leather's strength. It is the ability of leather to lengthen, or stretch, when stress is applied. At some point fibers will give way. Elongation of leather varies according to tanning and fat-liquoring procedures in its processing. Elongations as low as 15 percent and as high as 60 percent are possible. Gloves need high elongation because fingers flex and gloves are pulled over the fingers, but leather used for machinery belting needs to have very low elongation so it doesn't slip off its wheels.

Leather used for machinery belting requires very low elongation so it doesn't slip off wheels.

An interesting point about the network structure of leather's fibers is that in the belly area of a hide it is possible to "tease" fiber bundles as long as six inches, but not on the upper back of the hide.

The combination of these physical properties, with potential variations as indicated, makes a sheet of leather a rather remarkable material. Its properties, when understood, should also indicate what one can or cannot do with the material. Forcing a particular leather (considering tannage processes) to do what it was not processed to do invites failure. Conversely, understanding the material leads to success.

DEFINITION OF LEATHER

We now should have a general idea as to what leather is and what its potential is. Leather is the hide, or skin, of an animal (usually mammal or reptile) that has been preserved by dressing (tawing or tanning) into a stable, nonputrescible flexible sheet.

A WORD ABOUT FUR

Fur is dressed but processed differently than leather so that hair follicles are not destroyed. Fur often is used in conjunction with leather, usually as trim. The most important concept for us to know is that fur may also be glued, sewn, cut, pinned, joined, and attached much like leather. Care should be taken not to catch the short and long hairs of fur in sewing and that furs should be cut on the flesh side.

DISCOVERING TANNING DIFFERENCES

When you cut a piece of chrome-tanned leather and look at a cross section of it, you will see a bluish-gray streak in the center layer where coloring did not penetrate. Vegetable-tanned leather is more uniform in color.

Another test is to moisten the leather in warm water and then fold it. The vegetable-tanned piece will feel slippery but hold its crease, and the chrome-tanned piece will feel "drier" but spring back.

CLASSIFICATION IN TERMS OF KINDS OF SKINS AND HIDES

The following list was adapted from "Leather Facts," New England Tanners' Club, and indicates the name of the final product and what is available on the market.

ALLIGATOR
Alligator, crocodile, and related types.

BELTING
Usually supplied in a roll in round or flat narrow continuous stripping.

BUCKSKIN
Deer and elk skins, having the outer grain removed.

BULL HIDE
Hide from a male bovine, capable of reproduction.

CABRETTA
A hair-type sheepskin; specifically, those from Brazil.

CALFSKIN
Skin from a young bovine, male or female.

CAPESKIN
From a sheep raised in South Africa.

CARPINCHO
A water rodent native to South America; like pigskin.

CATTLEHIDE
General term for hides from a bovine of any breed or sex, but usually mature; includes bull hide, steerhide, cowhide, and sometimes kipskins.

CHAMOIS (see Flesher)
The product of oil tanning the underneath layer (called a "flesher") that has been split from a sheepskin.

CORDOVAN
From a section of a horsehide called the shell.

COWHIDE
Hide from a mature female bovine that has produced a calf.

DEERSKIN
Deer and elk skins, having the grain intact.

DIPLOMA
Usually vegetable-tanned sheepskin used in making diplomas.

DOESKIN
From sheep or lambskins, usually with the grain removed.

ENGLISH BRIDLE
A high quality cattlehide oak-tanned in a bridle-tanning process; excellent for tooling, sandals, and a wide variety of applications.

FLESHER
The underneath (flesh side) layer of a sheepskin that has been split off. Used to make chamois.

GLOVE
Sheep, pig, deer, and kidskin that has been tanned to produce a soft, stretchy leather for dress gloves. Also, cattlehide splits, sheepskin, and others that are tanned for garden and work gloves.

GLOVE HORSE
A supple horsehide used for garments given exposure to weather.

GOATSKIN
Skin from a mature goat.

HAIR CALF
Skin of a calf with the hair intact. When hair is clipped short it is called *hair calf clipped.*

HAIR SHEEP
Sheep from several species whose "wool" is hairlike.

HARNESS
Vegetable-tanned cattlehide leather finished for harness, saddlery, and sculpture.

HEIFER
A female bovine, under three years of age, that has not produced a calf.

HORSEHIDE
Hide from a horse or colt.

KANGAROO
From the Australian kangaroo or wallaby.

KIDSKIN
Skin from a kid, or young goat.

KIPSKIN
Skin from a bovine, male or female, intermediate in size between a calf and mature animal.

LAMBSKIN
Skin from a lamb, or young sheep.

LATIGO
Cowhide sides tanned with alum, gambier (a yellowish catechu), and oil. Used for saddle strings, lacing, carved forms, sculpture.

LINING
A shoe leather used for lining the inside portions. Made from all kinds of hides and skins, either grain- or suede-finished.

LIVE OAK
Vegetable-tanned cowhide producing a clear and even grain. Good for tooling, sculpture, and many other uses.

LIZARD
Any of a great number of the lizard family.

MOCHA
Middle East hair sheep, usually with the grain removed.

NOVELTY
Any of a variety of leathers, frequently vegetable tanned, used for billfolds and small leather goods.

OSTRICH
From the two-legged animal native to North Africa.

PATENT
Leather, heavily finished to give a highly lustrous, baked-enamel appearance, often used for shoe uppers. Generally from cattle-hide.

PECCARY
From a wild boar native to Central and South America; like pigskin.

PELT
An untanned hide, or skin, with the hair on.

PIGSKIN
Skin from pigs and hogs.

RAW STOCK
General term for hides, or skins, that a tanner has received in a preserved state pre-paratory to tanning; a tanner's inventory of raw material.

SADDLE SKIRTING
Very heavy cowhide sides vegetable tanned for saddles. Good also for sculpture.

SHARKSKIN
From certain of the shark species.

SHEARLINGS
Wooled sheep and lambskins, tanned with the wool intact with a nap of ¼ to ¾ inch.

SHEEPSKIN
Skin from a mature sheep.

SKIVER
The thin grain layer split from a sheep-skin.

SLUNK
Skin of unborn or prematurely born calf, tanned with hair left intact.

SNAKE
Any of a number of the snake species.

STEERHIDE
Hide from a mature male bovine, in-capable of reproduction, having been raised for beef.

SUEDE
Leather-finishing process whereby the flesh side or top of a split is buffed to produce a nap. Exceedingly difficult to tell kind of skin, or hide, used.

UPHOLSTERY
Large cattlehide, split thin, and tanned for use as furniture and automobile seat coverings.

WALRUS
Skin from a walrus; also, sometimes sealskin.

WATER BUFFALO
Flat-horned buffalo, primarily from the tropics.

CLASSIFICATION ACCORDING TO PARTS

BACK
Usually a side with belly cut off. In a hide it is usually 1,578 square feet per side.

BELLY
Underpart of hide, usually comes in two sections usually 6 to 10 square feet.

BELLY CENTER
The middle part of the belly with leg areas cut off, usually 3 to 5 square feet.

BUTT END
Unused or remaining portion of the hide such as the thigh area.

CROP
A side minus the belly portion.

CROUPON
The most ideal part of the hide, the back only minus the shoulder and belly.

EXTREME
A side just larger than a kip, but smaller than cow or steer sides; usually 17 to 20 square feet.

HIDE
The whole pelt from large animals such as cows, bovines, horses, buffalo; usually 44 to 52 square feet.

KIP
Skin from a bovine, either male or fe-male, before it reaches maturity in an inter-mediate stage; usually 8 to 10 square feet.

SHOULDER
Back-front part that wraps around from the back to the chest; usually 10 to 15 square feet.

SIDE

One half of a skin, or hide; from cowhide usually 22 to 26 square feet.

SINGLE BEND

Most ideal section—one half of the section of the back of a hide; usually 8 to 12 square feet.

SKIN

Pelt from small animals such as calves, sheep, goats, pigs, etc.

SPLIT

A layer of hide from under the top grain; sometimes splits are coated to make them look like top grain.

The Subdivisions of a Hide
This is the way hides from large animals are subdivided.

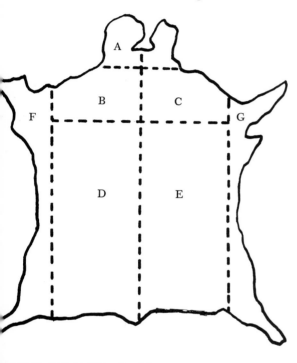

Head—A

Shoulder—B or C

Bend—D or E

Belly—F or G

Side—A+B+D+F or A+C+E+G

Crop—A+B+D or A+C+E

Back—B+D or C+E

Croupon—D+E

Courtesy New England Tanners' Club

HOW LEATHER IS SOLD

Hides are usually cut into smaller sections for easier handling. The way leather is sold varies. It is far from standardized. The tanner may sell it one way, the wholesaler another, and the retailer still another way.

Leather is priced by the square foot and is available in various thicknesses from one to twelve ounces or more. This designation means that one-ounce leather weighs one ounce per square foot; six-ounce leather weighs six ounces per square foot, etc. One-ounce leather usually is $\frac{1}{64}$ of an inch in thickness; six-ounce cowhide would then be $\frac{3}{32}$ of an inch. Ten- to twelve-ounce cowhide would be about $\frac{3}{16}$ of an inch thick. It leather is over ten ounces, it usually is sold by the pound.

Markings on hides are stated as 6^1, 6^2, 6^3, which means that it is $6\frac{1}{4}$, $6\frac{1}{2}$, and $6\frac{3}{4}$ square feet.

Other tanners classify hides according to "L" for lightweight, "LM" for light medium, and "H" for heavy. It is best to see a hide before buying it, until you get used to a certain supplier's nomenclature.

Don't insist on an exact square footage because it is not always available. Experienced leather craftsmen know that top grain leather generally will have flaws or scratches on it. You will have to accept that and work around it by either eliminating it from your cutting or incorporating it into your design.

Finally, no matter what classification is used, when ordering leather describe it whenever possible by kind, color, weight, grade, or quality, and size of skin or side.

HOW SOLE AND GARMENT LEATHER IS SOLD

Sole leather is measured by "irons." One iron is equal to a piece that measures $1/48$ of an inch thick. One sixty-fourth inch equals one ounce and $3/16$ inch equals nine irons or about twelve ounces. The thickness of most sandals is nine- to ten-iron leather, equivalent to twelve- to thirteen-ounce cowhide and about $3/16$ inch thick.

Garment patterns, on the other hand, require conversion from yardage. An easy conversion factor is if the pattern suggests a 36 inch width, multiply the yardage needed by nine. Then increase the yardage by multiplying your answer 15 percent to account for waste. If a pattern calls for 54-inch-width material, then use 13 as a conversion factor. Therefore, for a pattern requiring three yards of 54-inch material, $3 \times 13 = 39$; 39×15 percent $= 4.85$; $39 + 4.85 = 43.85$. You then need about 44 square feet of leather, if you round it off.

CONVERSION CHART

Ounces	Millimeters	Irons	Approximate Fractional Inches
1	.40	.75	1/64
2	.79	1.50	1/32
3	1.19	2.25	3/64
4	1.59	3.00	1/16
5	1.99	3.75	5/64
6	2.39	4.50	3/32
7	2.78	5.25	7/64
8	3.18	6.00	1/8
9	3.58	6.75	9/64
10	3.96	7.50	5/32
11	4.37	8.25	11/64
12	4.78	9.00	3/16

PROPER LEATHER FOR PARTICULAR PRODUCTS AND USES

Just as leather must be understood to know the range of its potential, so it is necessary to know which leathers will do the best job for a particular application. Even though specific properties of leather can be controlled to a certain extent by tannage, there are limitations caused by the architecture of the leather. The goatskin tanner cannot turn goatskin into calfskin because the underlying structures are unique and cannot be changed. This natural architecture puts limits on which products can be made from a particular leather, a testimony to the uniqueness of each leather.

The following list should provide an indicator and only that, of which leathers work best for certain products. There are always exceptions to common practice that turn out sensationally!

BELTS AND ANIMAL COLLARS

Seven to nine ounce; usually cowhide, pigskin, calfskin. The best material is English bridle back.

BRIEFCASES

Four to six ounce; heavy cowhide, latigo, steerhide.

FURNITURE (straps, suspended, sling)

Eight to fourteen ounce; cowhide, bovine, or any suitable top grain leather that has been processed to reduce stretch.

GARMENTS AND HATS

Two to three ounce; antelope, buckskin, chamois, garment suede (lambskin), split cowhide, doeskin, kidskin, pigskin, cabretta (sheepskin); the range is grains, splits, and suedes.

HANDBAGS

Generally four to ten ounce, depending on whether the leather is lined or is to be molded. Lambskin (garment suede), medium weight split cowhide, and some novelty leathers if lined.

LININGS (leather)

One to five ounce depending on what it is to be combined with and its use. Skivers, splits, suedes do best. Since some leathers stretch, buckskin and elk, for instance, lining is important to minimize stretching. It might be wise to design a seam in areas most likely to stretch, such as the knees in pants.

PILLOWS

Two to four ounce; buckskin, lambskin (garment suede), lightweight cowhide, pigskin, sheepskin (cabretta), goatskin, scraps of various sorts of leathers, top grain, and splits.

SANDALS

Bottom sole—eleven- to twelve-ounce oilbase leather with a fish-oil tannage. Top of sole—seven to eight ounce of curried (prestretched) leather, often medium weight cowhide.

SCULPTURE

Laminated, bent, and molded forms—ten ounce and up, vegetable tannage, usually cowhide, steerhide; skin coverings—two- to three-ounce vegetable tannage.

UPHOLSTERY

One- to four-ounce leather, curried (prestretched), and top-grain cowhide.

WALLETS AND KEYCASES AND SMALL PRODUCTS AND BOOKBINDINGS

Two to four ounce; pigskin, calfskin, cowhide, goatskin.

Specific information about kinds of leathers will be given for some of the projects that follow.

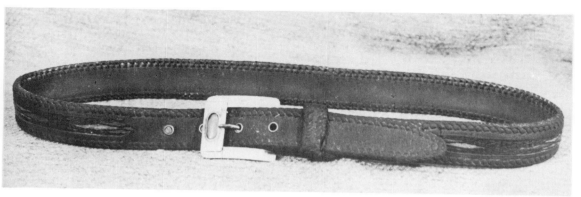

Spanish influence in trimming leather and Navajo in weaving is combined in this early twentieth-century belt that used horsehair in black, with white dyed red and yellow for its inset.

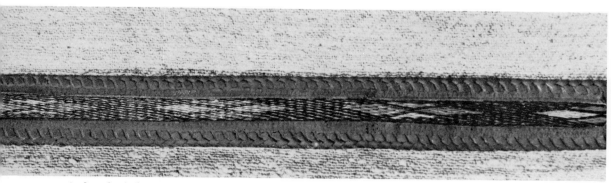

A detail of the belt showing the geometric horsehair weaving and its marriage with leather edged with a double "buttonhole" trim.

3

"Quartermastery": Tools and Their Uses

Leather can be worked in minimum conditions or, of course, in a workshop where every convenience is at hand. The only difference is that process is easier, but product excellence does not necessarily come from fancy tools and work spaces. I have seen beautiful products made on a tree stump in a shed, and ugliness come out of a first-class studio. For this reason all types of environments are depicted throughout this book as well as a wide variety of tools, from what we find around the house to those tools that are especially designed for leatherwork. Since leather has been around for a long time, the range of tools can be tremendous. All these tools, however, are not necessary. Leatherworking is one of the most inexpensive crafts to outfit, if you don't invest in machinery.

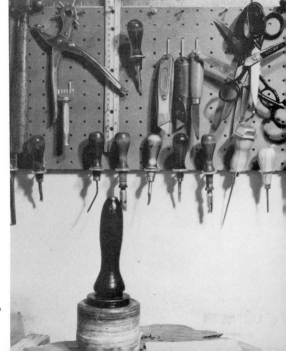

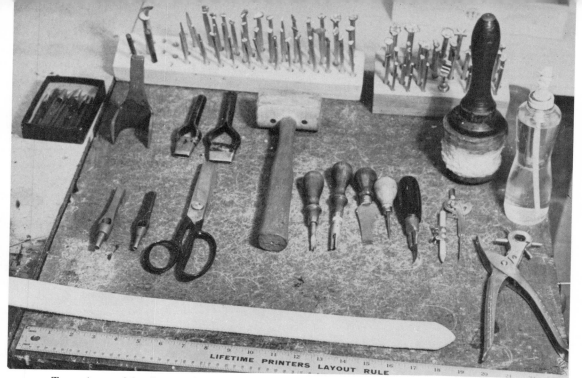

Two views of leather crafters' tools. John and June Anderson use a pegboard to organize tools and keep them within easy reach. John Giordano arrays his tools on a counter before he begins to tool a leather belt or pocketbook.

THE WORKING PLACE

A large area upon which you can lay out a hide for cutting patterns is important. It can be a dining table (with linoleum or several layers of cardboard to protect it), a floor, or a solid worktable in a studio. A smaller worktable that is really solid and will take hammering is also necessary. One of the most successful is a large size tree trunk that is the right height and level so that it does not rock. A butcher-block table would be great, too.

Some area should be available for the orderly assembly and storage of tools. Each tool should have its own place for quick retrieval. Supplies such as glues, polishes, edge coatings, and dyes must have clear markings and their own place on a shelf.

Two baskets or cardboard cartons, one for scraps you are saving and the other for garbage, should be at arm's length. Leather is a clean craft, though, with very little mess resulting from its operations.

There also should be a clean dry (but not hot) place to store your leather, preferably with skins and hides laid out flat or individually rolled and stored on their sides (not ends). And, since leatherworking is a precise art, there should be adequate lighting without cast shadows so you can see what you are cutting, stitching, etc.

BASIC TOOLS

If you gather together these materials, you can begin.

Sharp knife, preferably with a bevel edge—for cutting leather.
Shears, 7½ to 8 inches long and very sharp—for cutting leather.
Awl—for piercing holes for stitching.
Ball-point pen—for marking lines of patterns.
Ruler—for measuring.
Razor blades—for cutting and skiving.
Hammer or stick—for striking dies and pounding seams.
Mallet—water buffalo hide or hard rubber—for striking and fixing seams.
Brush—for applying edge coating.
Sponges—for applying dye, and wetting down leather.
Soft flannel or cheesecloth—for polishing and applying dyes.
Square—for measuring and getting right angles.
Revolving punch—for punching round holes for eyelets, lacing, etc.

Fork (eating fork with "sharpish" points)—for marking stitching holes and scratching parallel lines.

A PROFESSIONAL'S TOOL LIST

Leather shears (7½ to 8 inches)—has a serrated blade and razor-sharp edge to keep leather in place and to cut all thicknesses.

Bevel point knife—for cutting leather and skiving.

Scratch awl—for marking leather, piercing holes.

Square—for measuring and guide in cutting.

One-prong thonging chisel—for making slits for lacing, particularly at corners. Two sizes available: ³⁄₃₂ and ⅛ inch.

Four-prong thonging chisels—for cutting equally spaced slits for lacing. Several sizes available.

Revolving punch and combination punch—for punching round holes. Equipped with six different diameter dies; combination also sets eyelets.

Punches—drive, oblong, and English point—assorted, round, and oval—for punching holes of various sizes and types for belt buckles, straps, etc.

Snap-button tool—for setting of snap fasteners and eyelets.

Edge beveler, assorted sizes—for beveling of edges of different weights of leather.

Edge creaser—for marking a crease in leather to aid in folding.

Rampart gouger—for cutting grooves in heavy leather to aid in folding and stitching.

Mallet—rawhide, wood, or fiber—for striking dies, punches, eyelet setters; tapping seams.

Steel hammer—for tapping shoemaker tacks, etc.

Lacing needles (a flat shape)—for stringing lacing through thong slits.

Space marker—a wheel for marking spaces evenly for hand stitching.

Stitching punch—for punching uniformly spaced holes for hand stitching in light-medium-weight leather.

Fid—looks like an awl, used for enlarging holes, marking leather, aiding in lacing.

Draw gauge—for cutting heavy leather strips to preadjusted widths.

Harness needles, assorted—has an egg eye and blunt point.

Glover's needles—sizes four, five, and six—egg eyes and three-square sharp point for sewing lightweight leather.

Striking mallet—used for driving dies and stamps.

Lockstitch awl—for sewing medium to heavy leather with a lockstitch similar to the kind of stitch made on a sewing machine.

Head knife—for cutting and skiving heavy leather.

Skife—a metal handle containing a Schick injector razor blade used for skiving leather.

Skiving knife—a diagonal pointed beveled edge knife used for cutting and skiving.

Dividers—for marking spaces for stitching holes, drawing circles, and parallel lines.

Lacing pliers—for pulling heavy lace and reaching ends of lace between layers when lacing is completed.

Steel bar—upon which to place rivets for striking into the leather.

Edge slicker—a wheellike form containing a groove, run along edges for softening right-angle cuts into curved edges.

Bone folder and edge creaser—an edge slicker with a bone letter-opener type of blade for marking creases and lines, slicking edges, and aiding in curving folded leather edges.

Scraper—a prickly metal tool for roughing surfaces slightly so adhesives hold better.

Lasting pincers—looks like a narrower canvas stretcher for pulling leather over a last or mold in order to hammer a nail in place, usually with the flat end of the pincers.

Lacing pony—a vertical wooden "arm" that grasps an item, holding it while leaving both hands free for lacing.

One word about buying tools. If there is a choice between an inexpensive one and a good, solidly made tool, invest in the better one.

Certainly a basic and essential tool—the knife for cutting leather. Take care you don't cut your fingers.

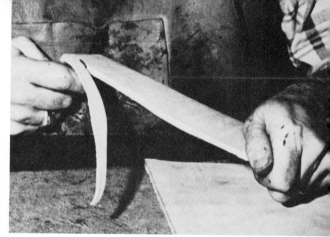

The head knife is used for cutting and skiving heavy leather. In this case it is used for skiving by pushing the knife away from you.

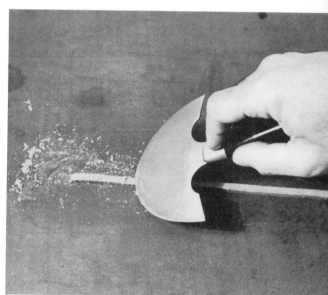

Sharpening the head knife on a sharpening stone, first on the rougher side, then on the finer side, using motor oil and rotating the knife as indicated in the diagram on the stone.

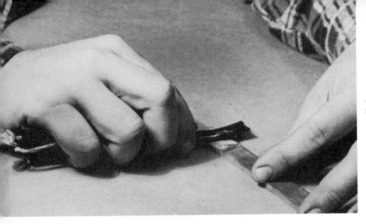

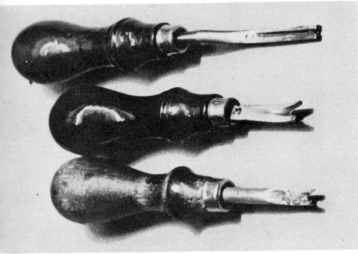

A skife uses a Schick injector razor blade for skiving leather.

Assorted edge bevelers.

An edge beveler in action.

Edge bevelers are used for refining corners and edges as in this belt flap.

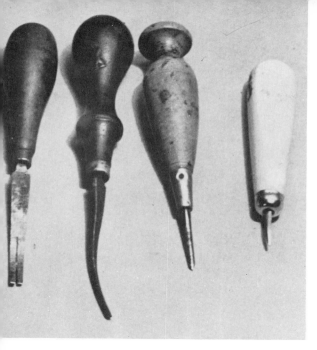

On the left is an edge beveler; next to it is a "V" groover, and the two tools on the right are awls.

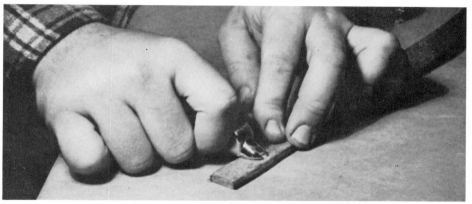

A rampart gouger used for cutting grooves in heavy leather to aid in folding and stitching.

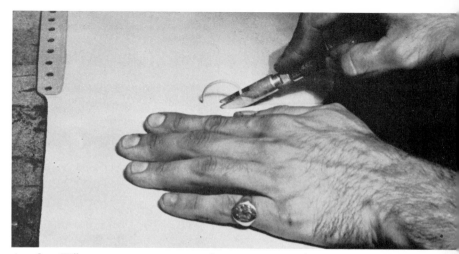

Another "V" groover, or gouger, used to cut away a sliver as in the rampart gouger so that a pocketbook flap can be folded.

Revolving thonging punch used to make holes for thonging and lacing.

The punch is used to make belt holes for a buckle.

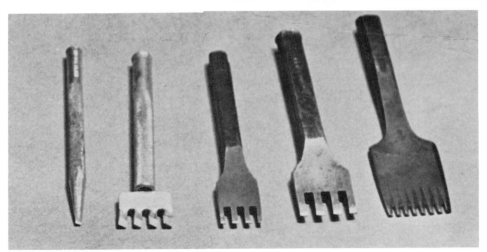

Assorted thonging chisels used to form various-sized slits in leather for threading thonging.

Assorted hammers.

One use for a hammer is to attach a rivet.

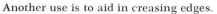
Another use is to aid in creasing edges.

On the left is a hardwood edge slicker and on the right is a style of mallet.

A brush is used to apply edge sealer. Cotton swabs can be used also.

Various punches, or dies, used for making different kinds of holes for thonging, and straps particularly.

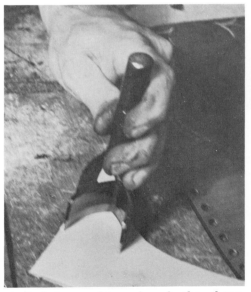

A die being used to make a leather shape.

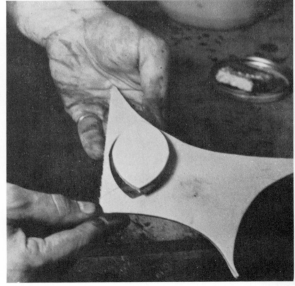

The resulting shape that is to be used as a "button" for a pocketbook closing.

A bone folder and edge slicker that is used for various purposes, particularly marking leather and rounding out edges.

A bone folder used to press or tool a design into the leather.

A scraper used to roughen leather surfaces before cementing and laminating one piece of leather to another permanently.

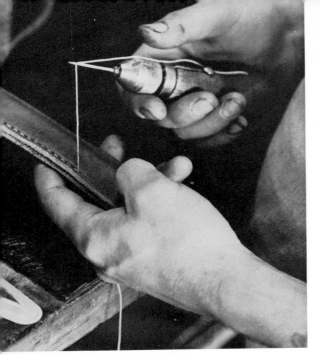

A lockstitch awl containing a needle and bobbin of thread for sewing medium to heavy leather with a lockstitch similar to a sewing machine.

TOOLS FOR CARVING AND MODELING

Modelers, assorted—with sharp points and various size ball ends for depressing outlines and areas and flattening edges.
Mallet—for striking stamps.
Assorted stamps with dies of various patterns.
Swivel knife—carving leather by excising lines.
Saddle stamps, assorted—decorating leather surfaces.

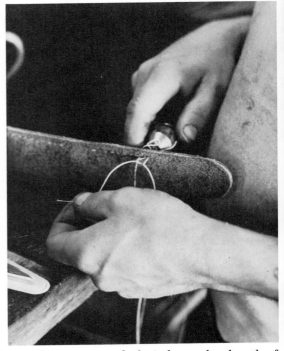

In order to create a lockstitch, another length of thread is threaded through loops made by the needle and thread which, in turn, is pulled from the bobbin.

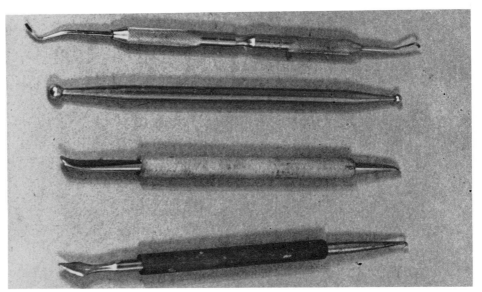

Modeling tools can range from old dental tools as seen at the top to assorted sculpture and metal repoussé tools below.

Wood-carving tools (chisels and cutters) can be used to sculpt areas of leather.

A swivel knife is used to carve leather by excising lines.

MACHINE TOOLS

(Some of these machine tools can be hand- or foot-powered. See entries with asterisk.)

*Sewing machine equipped with special roller "presser foot" (if possible) and heavy-duty motor.

Hand drill, buffer, sander—drilling holes, buffing and sanding leather.

*Skiving machine—skiving edges of leather.

*Pressure-riveting machine—attaching eyelets, grommets, rivets, closings of various kinds.

*Cutter—a revolving wheel cutter that cuts heavy leathers. Used particularly by sandalmakers for trimming sole of sandal around pattern.

*Splitting machine—splits layers of leather off a piece by pulling it through a roller and knife blade that is six inches or more in width.

Flexible shaft tool—handy because of the wide range of attachments you can use, from polishing to carving and incising.

Jigsaw, band saw, and saber saw—very useful for cutting any leather from five ounces up to the thickest parts.

Dies and the clicker—a clicker is an electric machine with a tremendous impact, or thrust. It can stamp dies of various patterns through thick leather. When many parts are necessary, e.g., for cutting many circles or many sandal soles, a clicker is used.

This sewing machine is equipped with a special roller "presser foot."

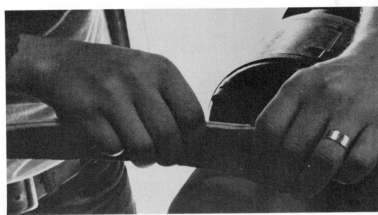

Hand drills or stationary drills are used for drilling, buffing, and sanding as illustrated here.

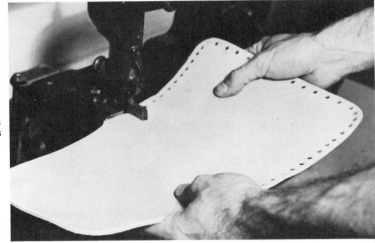

A skiving machine cuts away a portion of an edge or strap, depending upon its adjustment.

A skived edge performed by a skiving machine.

This pressure riveting machine attaches eyelets, grommets, rivets, snaps, depending upon the die that is applied.

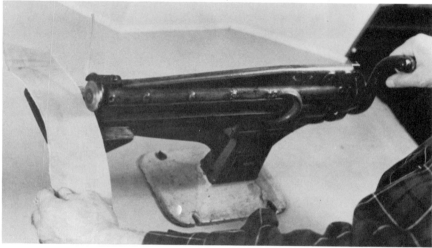

A cutter with a revolving wheel that cuts into heavy leather as if it were paper.

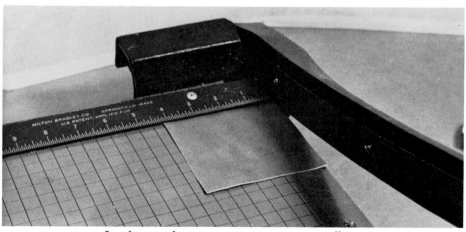

Leather can be cut on a paper cutter as well.

These are basic machines. There are, however, much more elaborate ones used in production work. Virtually every hand operation has been translated into a machine that will do the job, but not necessarily any better than a skilled craftsman. (I personally prefer the signs of handwork, indicated through deviations from sameness, even if it is a smear of glue, dye that shouldn't be there, or a hole that is not in exactly the same place as on the original model.)

BASIC SUPPLY AND FINDINGS LIST

Heavy leather or a Neolite sheet (see your shoemaker) for a cutting base to keep from dulling your sharp tools.

Threads of various kinds such as heavy-duty carpet thread, linen bookbinder's thread, waxed threads, cotton-covered Dacron.

Beeswax cake—for waxing unwaxed threads, for polishing.

Rivets, eyelets, snap fasteners, grommets— assorted sizes, varieties, and colors.

Buckles, loops and rings, dees (a metal ring in shape of a "dee" used for attaching straps).

Soling or cobbler's nails (like the shoemaker uses).

Leather cement—for gluing leather parts together and for fixing seams.

Rubber cement—for temporary attachment and for clothing seams.

Masking tape—for assorted odd jobs.

Ball-point pen—for outlining patterns and marking leather on the flesh side.

Marking pen—for outlining and drawing.

Heavy paper or Scorasculpture—for making patterns.

Dyes—for coloring leather.

Applicators and daubers—for applying dyes.

Edging coating for coating and sealing raw leather edges.

Rubber gloves—for protecting hands from dyes.

Plasti-Tak—for temporarily attaching pattern to leather.

Thonging, assorted colors and thicknesses as needed—for attaching parts of small items.

Leather, assorted kinds—as needed.

Saddle soap—for cleaning and conditioning full-grain leather.

Waxes and polishes—to protect top grain leathers.

All these items are not necessary for each project, but sooner or later you will be needing most of these supplies. Certainly all the tools listed are not necessary, but you should know that they exist.

The actual use of tools and materials will be described during the step-by-step processes of making leather items.

4

Basic Processes

Fundamental operations have come down to us through the centuries when tools were few and simple. There are several essential processes that are applicable to the most complex of projects when mastered. Processes in this chapter are basic to all leatherworking construction and are treated in the usual sequence used in making an item. More elaborate techniques will be covered further along in the book.

Incorporated into the following projects are fundamentals such as using patterns, cutting leather, shapes, straps, thongs; gluing, sewing, attaching rivets and fasteners; simple dyeing and sealing of edges; covering a box, and so on.

PATTERN MAKING

At the beginning of all leatherworking is the designing of the object. Strict considera-

tion must be given to the potentials and limitations of leather, and to the fundamental characteristics of the leather you are using. Sometimes you have the leather on hand and design a project to suit your leather; other times you will be selecting a particular type of leather in kind, weight, and color to carry out your design.

Some patterns are ready-made and can be purchased from craft and leather shops or through mail order. Clothing patterns are purchased wherever they sell sewing supplies and yard goods.

After you have sketched your design, make a paper model of it, folding the paper where necessary and using masking tape instead of glue to attach it. If you like something and want to copy it, study it carefully, take measurements and tracings of outlines to reproduce the form, and indicate where folds should go. Simple objects like belts usually do not require a pattern, unless the contours are complicated.

If you like your paper model, you are ready to make a pattern. Any paper can be used, but if you want to keep your pattern for a long period of time use bristol board, cardboard, or the material that I like best, Dennison's Scorasculpture. It is a cellulosic that cuts easily and does not bend around the edges after repeated tracings. It holds up.

Translate your paper model to the pattern board by making allowances for the thickness of your leather. A rule of thumb is to add twice the thickness of the leather to be used to the edges of the piece to be folded. This means that you will be adding one-eighth- to one-quarter-inch borders to the edges of your pattern.

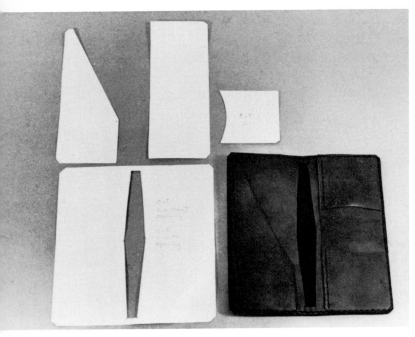

Translate your paper model to pattern board (from three dimensions to two), making certain that parts are marked.

Don Muller's wallet of 3½-ounce calfskin. Parts are attached with a lockstitch awl.

Mark each piece as it is cut, indicating which part it is such as strap, back, flap, gusset, etc. Also indicate on the pattern where fold lines go, where cutouts are, where straps are to be attached, and how many parts need to be cut. If a particular opening is unique, such as for a closing on a flap, or if there are to be lacing holes, carefully cut these out of the pattern so that you don't have to measure these areas each time. You merely will outline these shapes by tracing them on the leather. Note that when indicating lacing holes you have the same number of holes for pieces that are to be matched, else you may

end up with an extra hole here or there.

TRACING A PATTERN ON LEATHER

Wherever possible trace on the underside, or flesh side, of the leather. Arrange pattern parts so that you make the most economical use of the leather, but take note of any imperfections; avoid these. If you have pronounced grain, note variations and try to match areas where pattern parts meet. If you need to piece your leather, try to incorporate the piecing line into the design and play it to your advantage. Make an additional allowance here for overlapping of seams.

Professionals skip some steps as in Walter Dyer's factory by cutting around a pattern without the intermediate steps of tracing.

There are two ways to outline your pattern: by tracing it with a ball-point pen or by using a pointed instrument such as your dividers or bone folder/creaser to depress or scratch a line into the leather following the contours of your pattern. All the while keep

pressure on the pattern with your other hand to keep it from moving. If you use a flimsy paper, use bits of Plasti-Tak to temporarily attach pattern to leather. (See chapter 9 on clothing for the method of using Plasti-Tak.)

MAKING A CANDLE SLING

With a dividers, trace a 2-inch-diameter circle out of the center of an 8-inch square on the underside of the square.

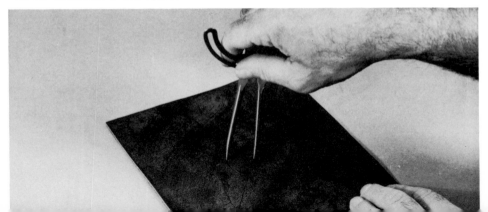

Next, with dividers draw a 4-inch-diameter circle in quarters leaving ½ inch between quarters. Then a 4½-inch-diameter with ½ inch between quarters, but leave these spaces halfway between the arcs of the previous circle. You will have four arcs completing the circle. Next, draw a 5-inch circle, alternating the ½-inch spaces, this time in the same position as the 4-inch circle. The last circle is 5½ inches in diameter with 1 inch between arcs, but with the arcs in the same position as the 4½-inch circle. The perimeter circle will be 6 inches in diameter.

With a razor blade or knife, cut around each line with a single cut. Only the center 2-inch diameter circle will fall free, along with the outside corners of the leather.

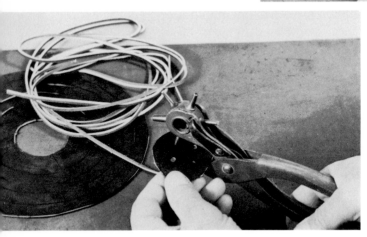

With a hole punch, press four holes of the proper size (to accommodate for ⅛-inch-wide thonging) into the 2-inch circle.

At four equidistant points along the outside edge (about ⅛ inch in from the edge), punch a hole. Each one should be positioned above an uncut point between the arcs.

Thread two thongs, each 6 inches long by ⅛ inch wide, in an "X" shape through the holes of the 2-inch-diameter piece.

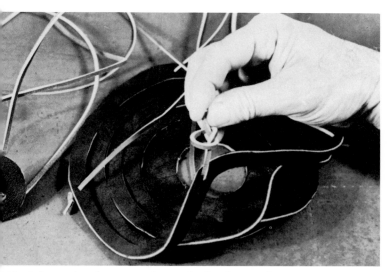

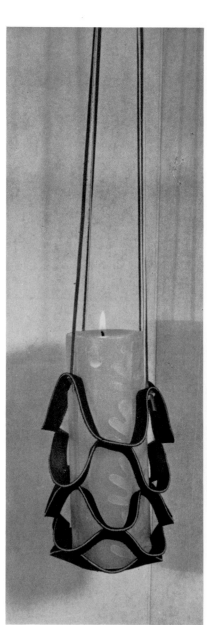

Straighten the thongs and attach the free ends through the holes in the sling, knotting them on the outside of the sling.

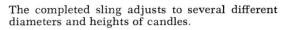

The completed sling adjusts to several different diameters and heights of candles.

CUTTING INTO LEATHER

You can use a very sharp knife, one that will not give you a ragged edge, or a leather shears. If the leather is a heavy weight, then use a band saw, saber saw, or shoemaker's cutting wheel. Place your leather wrong side (flesh) up on a heavy piece of leather, hard rubber, vinyl, or Neolite sheet, a material that does not have a grain, to keep your sharp cutting tools from dulling and catching. Place pattern pieces face side down on the leather. Or place your leather grain side up and the pattern on it face side up. Cut all straight edges with the aid of a steel ruler or L-shaped ruler. Curved lines need to be cut freehand. Hold the knife at a forty-five-degree angle and press down firmly and continuously as you draw around curves. Try to cut through the first time; it avoids ragged edges, but if necessary draw the knife along the same lines again until the cut is complete.

When using a scissors for small items, feed the leather into the scissors and keep the scissors in one position, steadily opening and closing the blades. If it is a large piece, while the pattern and leather are flat on the table, cut along the line using a slow, steady rhythm.

If you are using a saber saw, clamp your leather to keep it from moving. Cut all parts at the same time. You can label them if you need to with masking tape pressed on the flesh side. (Dyeing should be undertaken at the same sitting using the same batch, otherwise you will have variations in value because the water or alcohol would have had a chance to evaporate, making the dye mixture more intense in color.)

ED VIOLA'S POCKETBOOK

Along the outside edge of the pattern, trace a line, and also with an awl or dividers indicate, through holes in the pattern, where thonging holes should be located. This purse has a front, a front flap, a back, and a side gusset.

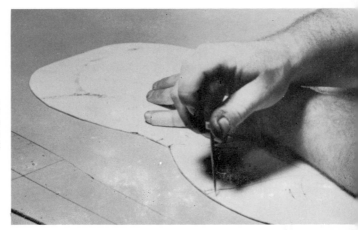

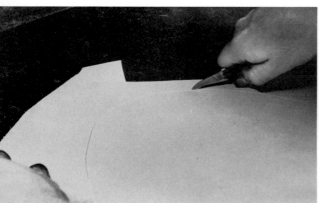

Cut along your outlines with a knife. Ed Viola is using a shoemaker's, or cobbler's, knife. The leather is five- to six-ounce latigo. Next, skive edges. Then cut two thonging lengths ½ inch wide and a 2-inch-wide strap.

With edge sealer (enamel or ink) coat the outside edges of your pieces.

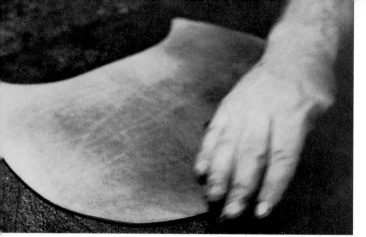

Apply dye. Ed is using a sponge in horizontal motions.

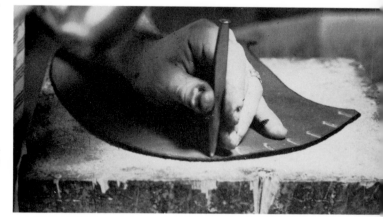

Following the thonging marks, cut thonging slits into the leather ⅛ inch from the edge using a ½-inch punch.

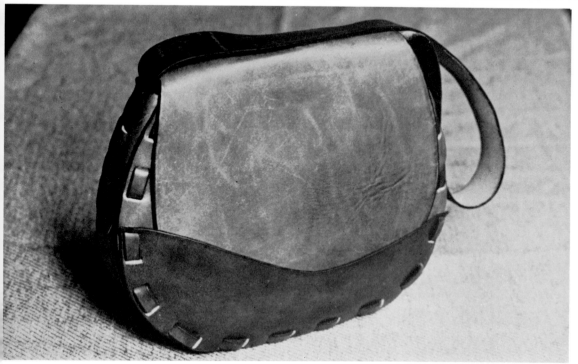

Thread thonging through the parts using a running stitch. Ed Viola's purse uses a "kangaroo" pouch to keep the lid closed.

Two purses by Walter Dyer using similar concepts of attaching parts. Notice that the purse lid uses slits and a strap for its closing. *Courtesy Walter Dyer*

LININGS

Linings usually are made of thinner leathers such as skivers, or thin splits of leather, garment suede, lightweight inexpensive leathers, or cloth. All leather objects do not need to be lined.

Cut linings the same size as the project pieces. Outline your pattern and use a leather shears to cut pattern pieces.

Leather linings are usually glued to the flesh side (wrong side) of the leather *after skiving*, if skiving is necessary. Cloth linings are sewn to key areas and are not glued. When gluing a lining, coat the leather (not lining) on the wrong side with a thin layer of rubber cement. Line up both pieces at one corner and then on one edge, and press the rest into place unrolling the lining while smoothing out any trapped air pockets. If rubber cement oozes out, let it dry before you pick it up with a ball of dry rubber cement or by rubbing it with your fingers. Do not try to remove rubber cement when wet; it sometimes embeds into the leather.

If you are lining heavy leather, and a groove has been cut into the leather to aid in the folding, use glue on both the heavy leather and on the lining in the area that is to be folded. Let the rubber cement dry a few minutes before placing one half to the groove, smooth that half, then fold the heavy leather,

and attach the rest of the lining while the leather is folded. If you attach it while the leather is laying flat, the lining will wrinkle. Then smooth away bubbles.

When lining suede with suede, use glue on both pieces.

SKIVING

If several leather edges have to meet or overlap, they form a great deal of bulk. In order to minimize this thickness, edges are thinned out by cutting, or *skiving*, away excess leather. For example, thonging ends are skived before attaching to more thonging. Skiving is also performed where edges have to bend, or fold, such as in the buckle area of a belt. Reducing thickness makes leather more pliable and also thins two thicknesses to that of one. Skiving is not usually necessary on lightweight leathers under three ounces.

Skiving is done normally on the flesh side, with a very, very sharp knife, steady pressure, and some forearm muscle. There are special skiving knives; the skife and the head knife work well, or you can even use a safety razor blade. The difficulty in skiving is to thin the leather enough without cutting unwanted holes or uneven edges.

Hold your leather firmly on a hard, steady surface. Marble or a lithograph stone is great. Usually skiving begins about one-half inch from the edge on the flesh side. Place the blade of your knife almost flat on the leather, then ease it up to a very shallow angle, and push the knife away from you, maintaining a steady pressure while working outward toward the edge. (The skife, though, is pulled toward you.) Cut shallowly to begin with; you always can cut off another sliver. Continue making small cuts until the desired depth has been obtained, while keeping an even one-half- to three-quarter-inch distance from the edge.

EDGING, BENDING, FOLDING, AND CREASING

EDGING

Edges are put on leather to impart a finished look or to dress a cut. It is not necessary to edge leather under six ounces because thin leathers don't seem to need it. Belts, handbag flaps, sculpture, sandals, boxes, usually look better when edged because any feathery excess or unevenness is trimmed away.

An edge cutter is used to perform this job. It comes in various sizes. Numbers two through four are the most useful. The tool rounds off edges by cutting off a sliver, beveling an edge.

Place the edge on a flat surface grain side up and push the tool along the edge away from you in one continuous stroke until you reach the end of that edge. For very heavy leather turn it flesh side up and repeat the operation. Some people finish their edging by rubbing it with a bone folder/creaser or a circle-edge slicker. Both have a U-shaped groove to burnish the edge into a smooth, slick surface. You must run the groove back and forth along the edge until a shine develops. All fuzzy fiber ends should disappear.

Next, with a paintbrush, cotton swab, pipe cleaner, or dauber, apply edge dressing, wiping off excess before application. Dark brown or black are the usual edge dressing colors. Take care not to run the dressing over onto the grain or flesh sides. It looks sloppy.

This edge dressing process can be performed before or after the grain surface has been dyed.

BENDING, FOLDING, AND CREASING

These are basic operations common to most projects. Bending, folding, and creasing avoids extra seams and utilizes whole pieces of leather. It is necessary to bend, fold, and crease leather so that it permanently stays in that position or returns to that position when desired. Bends usually are up to 90 degrees, folds are between 90 degrees and 180 degrees, and creases are over 180 degrees when the leather folds back on itself.

Leather under three ounces can be easily folded and creased. Leather above that, four ounces and up, needs some help. Dampening the leather will help to maintain a bend line and make the leather easier to bend. Carving a U or V groove on the flesh side along the line you wish to bend helps to fold and crease and will fix permanently the bend, fold, or crease. Cut the groove with a stitching groover, or a wood-grooving/carving tool. Cutting out a thin sliver of leather aids in folding by reducing bulk at the bend point. Take care not to weaken the leather at the fold by gouging out too much.

For leather over six ounces, lubricate the bending area on both sides with Vaseline so that cracking does not occur. On creases that are to be glued, use a bone folder to press the edge. Or, pound the crease with a mallet or a steel hammer. Make certain that the leather is damp or lubricated before doing this. Most garment leathers have the resilience to crease easily. Certainly leather under three ounces will cause no problems. Use props, weights, or a vise, if necessary, to maintain a bend, fold, or crease while the leather is drying out from water or glue.

LACING HOLES AND THONG SLITS

MARKING SEAMS

In order to maintain an even line parallel to an edge, take your dividers, adjust it for the depth from the edge that you want. Allow one point to travel along the outside with the edge acting as a guide while the other point marks the line. You can also use ruler measurements to draw a line.

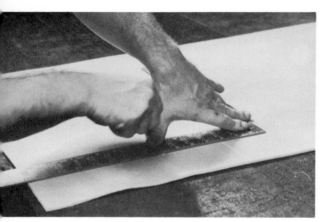

ED VIOLA'S BRIEFCASE

The measurements for Ed Viola's briefcase are 16 inches wide by 12 inches high by 4 inches deep. Each unit on the pattern diagram indicates 2 inches.

Ed does not use a pattern but prefers to measure off this simple pattern with an awl for marking and a right-angle square for measuring . . .

. . . as well as a steel ruler (directly on the leather). The leather is eight- to ten-ounce latigo. The measurements are laid out the longest length from head to tail so that the flap of the briefcase hangs properly, so Ed says. Parts are cut with a cobbler's knife.

Using an edge creaser and a right-angle ruler as a guide, he cuts out a sliver on the skin side so parts will fold easily.

Corners are cut away.

Edges are beveled, but not skived, because they meet and do not overlap.

The creases are folded.

He cuts a 3-inch-wide strap long enough for the closing and an over-the-shoulder handle strap using a draw gauge. After starting a cut into the leather, the leather is attached to a vise, the knife edge of the draw gauge is inserted in the slit, and then pulled along the edge of the leather, producing an even strap width.

Edges of the strap that will fold back on itself are skived in a skiving machine.

All edges are coated with an edge coater (black in this case).

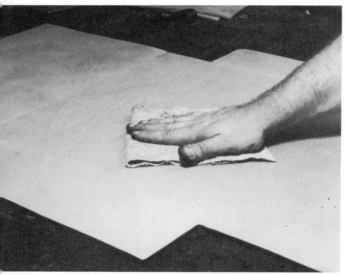

In preparation for dyeing, the surface is wiped clean with a dry Turkish towel. This process removes excess oil and allows for a more even application of dye.

Ed Viola mixes his own color (browns in this case), using powdered aniline dye and Synasol alcohol. (Two ounces to one gallon of alcohol is the proportion given.) He applies the color with a Turkish towel in a circular motion, exerting even pressure that never stops until all the color is spread out evenly on the grain side. He applies color two or three times with quick continuous motions until the color looks even. All pieces are dyed at the same time.

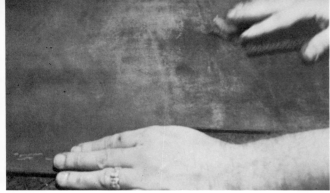

Then with a different, dry towel, he rubs off excess dye. Ed does not color the skin side because it rubs off.

Next with a bag punch he stamps out a hole for the strap closing and coats that edge with a cotton swab.

An awl marks the spacing for thonging holes. He uses an odd number of holes on one side because he uses a single stitch at corners.

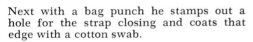

Holes of the proper gauge are punched along the edge.

All parts are waxed with Mel-O-Wax.

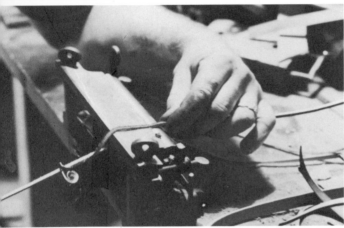

Thonging is cut with a draw gauge and then skived on the skiving machine to about two-thirds of its original thickness.

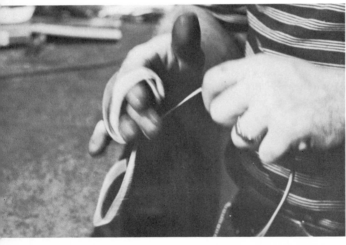

Ed Viola wraps the thonging into a ball in preparation for dyeing . . .

. . . and then immerses the thonging in the same dye he had used to dye the latigo. It is removed when the proper color depth develops and then is allowed to dry.

Meanwhile, he lines up holes to holes.

A knot is tied to one end of the thonging and a point is cut on the other end to facilitate threading. Without a lacing pony, parts are laced. New laces are not glued together, but rather a knot is placed in the final end as well as in the new piece and started the same way as the first one.

A double-ring closing is attached with a strap. Holes had been punched previously. The strap is slipped into place.

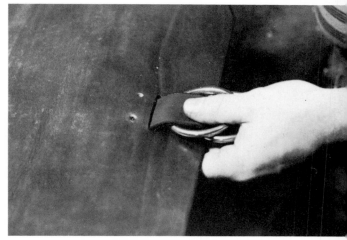

Rivets are used to attach all strap parts.

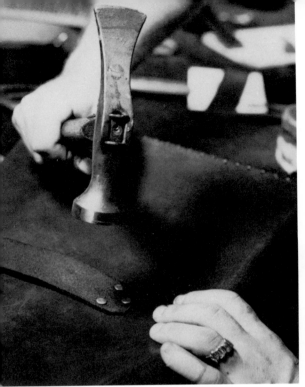

Rivets are used to attach all strap parts.

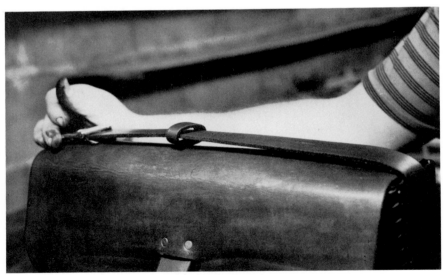

The handle is adjusted and its buckle is attached.

Another smaller version of a briefcase by Jeff Slaboden, using a brass-buckle closing and parts attached with hand stitching.

Ed Viola's briefcase, which really belongs to me. I love it!

MEASURING LACING HOLES

Stitches usually are evenly spaced. If you are to use a thong chisel, then the spacing will be automatic, as you will see, but if you are going to punch holes, then distances between holes need to be marked. To do this, you can use a ruler and at prescribed even intervals press the point of your divider or awl into the seam line you had drawn. Or, in a more automatic way, use a marking wheel, or stitch gauge, to indicate spacing. The stitch gauge is a wheel with points at set intervals. By running the wheel along the marked line, dots will be left by the pressure of the wheel, setting distances. Use a straight edge as a gauge. You can also dance a divider along the marked line by swiveling it on the line, each time keeping one point on the last mark. An alternative is to press marks with a fork.

PUNCHING HOLES FOR SEWING OR LACING

FOR HAND SEWING

If you are to sew light to medium leather, then it is best to use a stitching punch that has uniformly spaced holes. By holding the tool vertically and pounding the top of the tool with a mallet into the leather (over your leather, Neolite, or rubber base), you will have small prepared holes. Overlap

the chisel in the last hole, so that spacings between chisel holes are even.

You can also make holes with the needle of an unthreaded sewing machine by pretending to sew the edge. Or you can drill individual holes with an electric drill equipped with a very fine drill bit, the finest you can find. If the leather is heavy, groove out a shallow stitching line and follow the above operations.

FOR THONGING AND LACING

Thonging can be almost any width that is manageable for sewing two parts together. It is usually flat. Lacing is sometimes rounded at the edges and comes in narrower widths from $3/32$ to $3/16$ inch.

When using thonging, make thonging slits with a thonging chisel by pounding the chisel as described above along the marked line overlapping the last hole to maintain evenness. Chisel sizes should match the width of your thonging. Use a single thonging chisel around corners. For extrawide thonging, use a die that is used for attaching belts. Called a bag punch, it is a slitlike shape.

For lacing, you can use a rotary punch that has adjustable hole dies. Select the die that matches the width of your lacing and proceed to squeeze the punch at each mark that you have previously made. Thonging chisels are also useful.

Drive chisels or punches are used for larger widths.

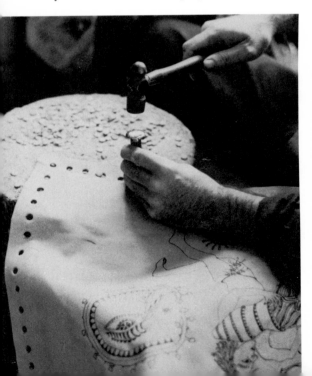

Jean Pierre Larochette punches thonging holes using a tree stump as a base.

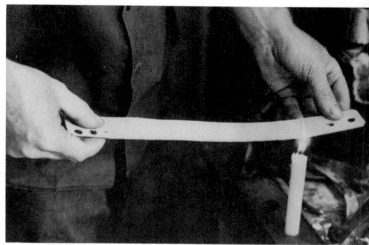

He singes off strands from the flesh side of the leather with a candle flame.

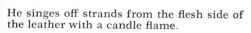

Jean's wife, Yael-Lurie, applies cement to the top edge of the leather, which is to become a sack.

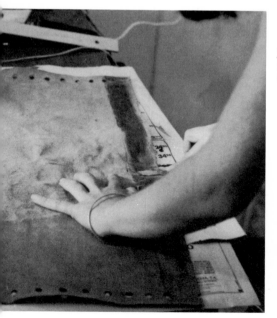

After drying for at least fifteen minutes, the leather is folded back on itself . . .

. . . and then pounded with a hammer.

Jean threads the thonging through the holes back and forth in a running stitch.

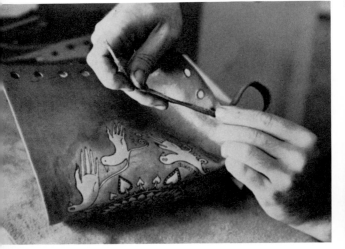

After stitching is used to attach all parts, the base edges are cemented.

Yael-Lurie and Jean Pierre Larochette's designs on purses.

Another sack by that talented team. Colors vary from a warm brown-orange hue to cool brown-blacks.

HOLES FOR STRAPS, AND RIVETS, GROMMETS, AND EYELETS

Rivet and eyelet holes can be made with a revolving hole punch unless they are too deep into the design; then a chisel punch of the proper size should be used. This is the case for strap holes and any other insertions. Some shapes may be nonstandard and would have to be cut out by knife.

CUTTING THONGS AND STRAPS

Thonging, or lacing, that is made from the same leather as the project makes for a more integrated piece because the dyes, for one, will take the same way; therefore, thonging, or lacing, blends to the point of belonging.

Cutting thonging from light to medium leather can be accomplished with leather shears, paper cutters, or a sharp knife. Thicker leathers require a knife or a draw gauge. Draw gauges cut even strips of leather for thongs, straps, belts, and other narrow parts from one quarter to four inches wide.

To use a draw gauge, begin your cut by holding the leather and forcing the blade into it. Then insert the blade and attach both parts of the strip into a vise and proceed to pull the draw gauge toward you until you have cut the length you want.

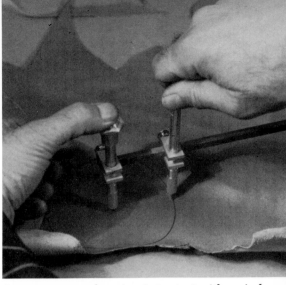

One way to cut thonging is to start with a circle. This circle cutter (X-acto), both a compass and a knife, is slicing a circle from the leather.

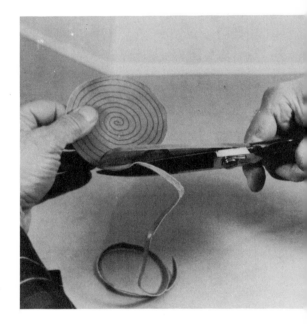

Then with a leather shears, an even cut is made, spiral fashion, to end up with thonging.

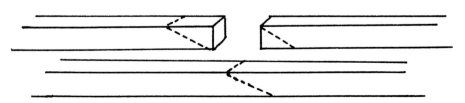

When thonging requires joining (when knots would be unsightly), they can be spliced and glued as illustrated.

DYEING AND FINISHING

Although dyeing and finishing of leather will be detailed in chapter 5, the most fundamental operations will be covered here. Dyeing and finishing follow in sequence after the above operations.

Most leathers used for handcrafting come in neutral tans or yellows (for latigo and chrome-tanned "latigo" hides). The yellow accepts dyes well. Leather can be dyed using the whole skin or only the cut portion of the pattern. Dye can be applied to natural finishes or over tannery-dyed leather as well.

Undyed leathers are porous and will absorb dyes readily, although sometimes unevenly, particularly if there is an imperfection in the hide.

Most commercial dyes are water soluble, or oil and spirit soluble. These liquids penetrate deeply into the pores of the grain. Dyes tend to stiffen the leather. That is why you should dye after holes are made for lacing, rivets, thongs, etc. It is easier. Dyes also fill the holes and help to cover raw edges. Dye before attaching metal parts and dye all leather attachments at the same time.

Make certain that the grain side of the leather is free of all greasy matter and dirt. You can wipe it clean with a soft, dry cloth and that is soft enough. If there is cement or stubborn dirt remaining, mix a mild solution of oxalic acid, one part to forty parts water. It comes out to about one teaspoonful of oxalic acid to a pint of water. Gently sponge this solution over the entire surface, but don't flood the area. Let the cleaner dry slightly before proceeding to dye.

Protect your work area with newspaper or plastic, and wear rubber gloves before dyeing to keep the dye from staining your hands.

Stir your dye and select your applicator. It can be a dauber for small areas, or a Turkish towel or piece of sheep wool for large surfaces. Try dyeing a small piece of leather first to practice and to judge for color depth. Always begin with the lighter color first, if you are to overlay colors.

Edging can also be colored (not sealed though) with an indelible black or dark brown marking pen. It's a short cut.

Different effects are created by the implement and the method of applying your dye. The first application takes best. Overlapping darkens areas. A quick sweep in a left to right application that distributes dye in equal quantities by overlapping of strokes will produce the most even effect. Applying dye in a circular overlapping motion will produce some pattern and more streaking. Make certain that the dye is accessible, will not drip on the leather surface, and that enough dye will saturate your Turkish towel or sheep wool quickly so that one area does not dry too long before you reapply successive first coats.

Frequently, the first dye coat is uneven. Go over it two or three more times to even out the coating. Dye your straps and laces and any other attachments now, using the same dye, same number of applications, and same implements for applying the dye.

SEWING AND LACING

HAND SEWING

I personally think that hand sewing is more attractive and stronger than machine sewing. Machine sewing, though, will be covered in chapter 9 on Clothing.

In sewing light to medium weight leather, you can rubber cement edges together to keep them from slipping. Mark a sewing line on the grain side the proper distance from the edge of your piece—usually $\frac{1}{16}$ inch with a dividers or another pointed instrument. Figure out how many stitches

per inch you will be needing to effect a secure seam. If you require twelve or more stitches per inch, you must use a fine needle and fine thread. The usual spacing for lightweight leather is eight to twelve stitches per inch.

Mark the stitching intervals with a stitching punch, awl, dividers, etc. Depending on the thickness of your leather, you may or may not need to prepare holes first before sewing begins. You will have to try it out to judge the resistance of the leather.

Select the proper size needle. Special leather hand-sewing needles are sold in leather shops, Singer sewing centers, and Tandy's. The diamond-point full-grooved needle is easiest to use, and is available in various sizes. The next requirement is choosing the proper thread. The type of thread used will be determined in part by the type of project and wear expectancy. A fine thread could be a polyester-covered cotton (Dacron), heavy-duty cotton button and carpet threads, silk and nylon, and waxed threads. Linen thread used for bookbinding is also good for fine work. For ornamental work a heavy silk buttonhole twist thread is the most attractive. In Mexico an incredibly strong thread is made of maguey (henequen) and is hand twisted. Threads that are not prewaxed need to be waxed by running the thread along the edge of a beeswax cake. The wax coating adds strength, minimizes abrasion, and makes it easier to sew. If you have a choice of threads, choose the heavier.

Stitches may vary from a plain running stitch, combination back stitch, overcast, to cobbler's and saddler's stitches that use two needles. (See the diagrams for details.)

Some Hand Stitches

a. The overcast stitch.

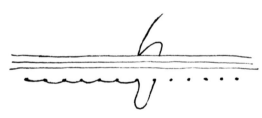

b. A plain running stitch.

c. A backstitch, which is reinforcing because it repeats itself through the same holes.

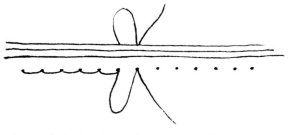

d. A cobbler's stitch when two needles are used.

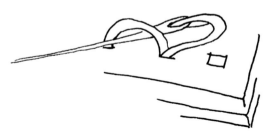

e. An enlarged cross section of a cobbler's stitch showing a lock-crossing of the thread . . .

f. . . . you thread the needles through the previous stitch.

Sewing medium to heavy leathers requires similar treatment as for lightweight leathers, except that you may not need to cement the edges together. But you should mark your sewing line and stitch distances. If the leather is very heavy, you may want to cut a groove for stitching. (This also lowers the level of stitching and doesn't expose the threads to abrasion.) Punching premade holes is important for heavy leathers. You can use an awl, a 1/16-inch electric drill for a #000 harness needle, or a stitching punch if it will penetrate through your leather thicknesses. Select your thread and be certain to wax it if it does not come that way.

After you stitch your leather with the selected stitch, tie the two ends together; place a small amount of cement on the knot and tap it into place with a hammer.

To use a *lockstitch sewing awl*, follow the instructions that come with the sewing awl. The thread needs to fit in the groove of the needle as it is threaded from the bobbin.

Keep tension consistent and the position of the thread in the same direction for even results.

A lacing pony is an aid in stitching because it frees both hands by clamping the project in place while you are lacing or sewing. Some lacing ponies are attached to benches; others require bracing between thighs.

LACING AND THONGING

Lacing and thonging are thicker and wider than thread and oftentimes stronger. They are at the same time both functional and decorative. Lacing and thonging stitches can contribute a "plus" to the design. Lacing usually is from $3/32$ to $3/16$ inch wide, is often curved at the edges, and usually comes in

rolls or hanks. Lacing is usually sewn with lacing needles, particularly if the holes are just slits. *Florentine*, or *Venetian*, *lacing* is softer and wider than other laces. It is meant to completely cover the edges of a seam and is used most often for albums, book covers, desk pads, and picture frames. It is generally cut from kidskin and comes in either $1/4$ or $3/8$ inch widths. A #0 punch is used to make holes for the $1/4$-inch lacing and a #1 punch for the $3/8$-inch lacing. Both holes are narrower and gather the lacing at the hole, while allowing it to fan or spread out around the edges. Each overcast stitch should overlap the previous one just slightly. To cover corners, sew two to three stitches in one hole—enough to completely cover the edge. And to finish lacing, run both ends of lace under two or three stitches on the back and cut off extra lengths.

A running stitch using thonging. Note knots for beginning and ending thonging.

Walter Dyer's pocketbooks are held together with a running stitch.

Thinner lacing stitches are quite varied and can be as simple as a running stitch, an overcast (whipstitch), or a single buttonhole stitch to very complex stitches that involve braiding concepts. Lacing can be accomplished with one or two needles. For details of some basic stitches see the diagrams and photographs.

When lacing is completed, a light pounding with a hammer or mallet gives the lacing an even appearance.

Thonging, because of its width, usually works best with very simple stitches, usually no more than a running stitch. Narrower thonging could be manipulated into overcast (whipstitch) or a cross-stitch. Thonging requires no needle because it usually is thicker and more rigid than the other joining materials.

Some Lacing Stitches

1. A simple overcast stitch. Corners are turned usually by stringing the lacing two or three times in the same hole.

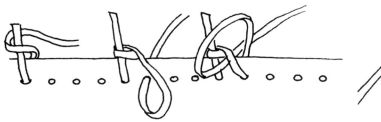

2. Three steps (from left to right) in making a single buttonhole stitch. Note that in the top view the stitch moves principally in one forward direction.

3. A simple cross-stitch first uses every other space in one direction and then reverses itself filling in the skipped spaces while crossing the other stitches.

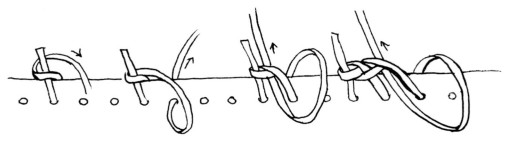

4. Four steps in making a double buttonhole (or double layover) lacing. Note that the lacing returns on itself as seen in the top view.

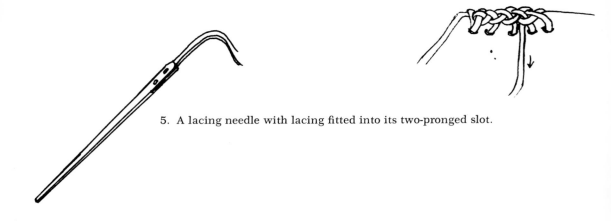

5. A lacing needle with lacing fitted into its two-pronged slot.

Justo Santa Anna Mancera adds a hat block to a hat he has just sewed together in preparation for trimming it with lacing.

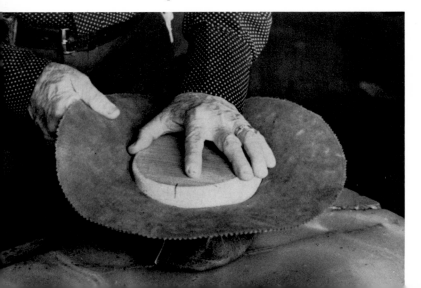

With dividers he marks the lines where lacing is to go.

Using a die, he pounds holes into the rim. The hat die acts as a backup base.

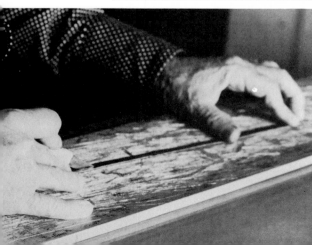

With knife and nary a ruler, he slits a strip of leather into the proper width of lacing . . .

. . . and proceeds to make an angled overcast stitch.

The completed gaucho hat (used to complete a riding habit) by Justo Santa Anna Mancera.

WET AND DRY BONDING

Sewing, lacing, and thonging are some ways of attaching leather parts; other ways are bonding or gluing and use of metal mechanical fasteners (see following section).

Whatever is not attached with thread, lace, or metal is bonded with glue. It is indispensable and can be quite permanent on forms that cannot be stitched or mechanically attached. Some of the projects that require building up of layers of leather are laminated pots, sandal soles, and other forms like sculpture and collage, and those techniques that utilize dissimilar materials along with leather. Most projects require some type of gluing.

There are two types of bonding agents: wet and dry. Wet bonding agents are applied to one or both surfaces and the parts are adhered while the glue or cement is still wet. These include epoxy cement, Duco cement, Testor's glue, Elmer's glue, Sobo, Quik, and other white glues that are vinyl-based. These glues permit moving around of the parts until the pieces are aligned. The vinyls (white glues), waterproof when dry, wash off with water when still wet. Epoxy, Duco, Testor's, and other similar glues stain, are not flexible, and are more difficult to clean off.

Dry bonding agents require coating of both surfaces, waiting until the glue is not tacky to the touch, and then accurately adhering both parts together. Barge and Masters, both manufactured specifically for leather, are dry bonding agents. Goodyear High Speed Neolite All Purpose Cement, Elmer's Fast Dry Cement, and Tandy's "Craftmen" All Purpose Cement are other good leather cements.

Rubber cement falls in either the wet- or dry-bonding category, depending upon whether parts are adhered while the rubber cement is wet or when both parts are dry.

Selecting a bonding agent depends upon the function of your article and which adhesive properties are most suitable. If a garment is to flex, then you require a flexible material such as rubber cement. If it is to be in contact with water, then Masters or Barge would be best. If leather is to be adhered to a hard nonporous surface such as glass or metal, then epoxy would work best. If beads or leather strips are to be inlaid into a surface, and the adhesive has to be applied very sparingly, then the white glues (vinyls) should be utilized because excess can be washed away quickly.

For projects that require strong bonding, bonding strength can be increased by roughing up the surfaces to be joined with a wire brush, coarse steel wool, sandpaper, a knife, or a file. This permits deep penetration of the adhesive.

Finally, tapping the bond with a mallet will eliminate air pockets and force a better contact. Applying a consistent pressure with weights or a press is also excellent.

Apply glues and cements with whatever works best—tongue depressor or popsicle stick, applicator stick or toothpick, brayer, cardboard, or brush. If you use a brayer or a brush, make certain that there is a solvent available to clean off the tool after use.

METAL MECHANICAL FASTENERS

Fasteners of various sorts—nails, rivets, and loops—are to permanently attach parts. Some permit parts to be removable, such as snaps and zippers. These parts are called *findings*. Findings should be designed into the projects and not become an afterthought. A misplaced finding can ruin an otherwise excellent design.

Fasteners can also be innovative. A door latch can be used as an opening of a leather (heavy) case; bones and parts of animal horns can be utilized as pocketbook and button closings; bobbins, large nails, clothespins, small pulleys, acrylic balls and dowels, and small pieces of driftwood can become innovative fasteners. Let your imagination swing freely.

As with any fastening device, the choice of a particular fastener is made because it will function the very best way for the item.

COBBLER'S, OR CLINCHING, NAILS

Cobbler's, or clinching, nails (extra iron) are small metallic blue-gray-black nails with a fine slightly curved point at the end. When you hammer a cobbler's nail into leather, it is exceedingly difficult to pull out. A metal base is needed. When you hammer these nails through the leather, they hit the metal base and curve back into the leather in a locking grip.

ED VIOLA'S PIPE RACK

Ed is cutting two free-form shapes, the same shape and size, from ten- to twelve-ounce leather.

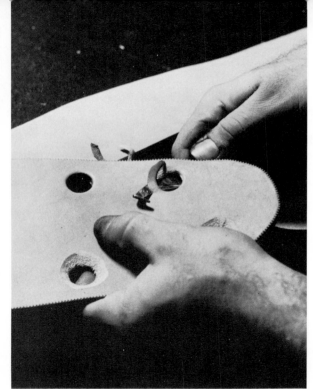

With a punch, he is at first indicating where holes will be in the top layer. Then he punches them out.

Holes are carved into a bevel.

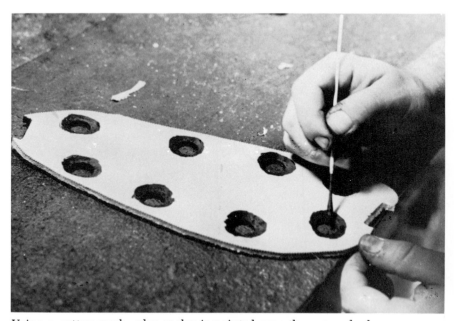

Using a cotton swab, edge sealer is painted over the exposed edges.

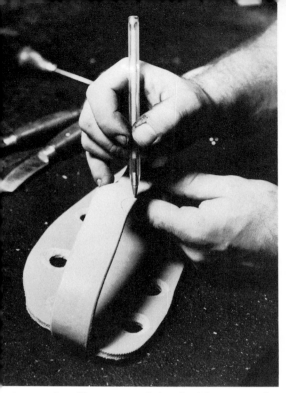

A strap handle is cut and fitted with grooves for pipe handles.

An edge beveler is refining all the edges of the handle.

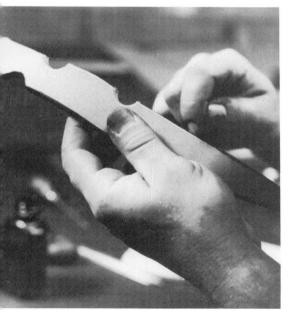

Edge sealer is used to coat all edges.

All exposed parts are dyed using a Turkish towel scrap that has been saturated with dye. Ed Viola uses rotating, overlapping strokes.

Cobbler's nails are used to attach the handle to the top section of the rack.

Barge cement is coated on both skin sides of the two-part base and allowed to dry for fifteen minutes.

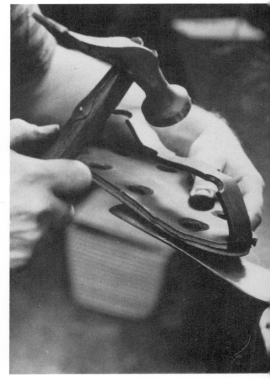

They are matched together and then pounded with a hammer.

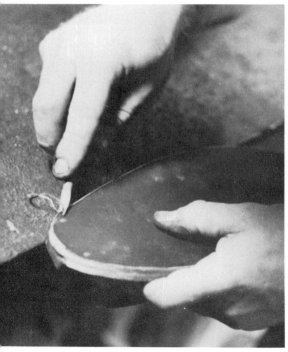

Outside edges are skived with an edge beveler.

The edge is sanded on a sanding wheel and then ink is used to dye the edge. The entire piece is waxed and buffed.

Ed Viola's pipe rack.

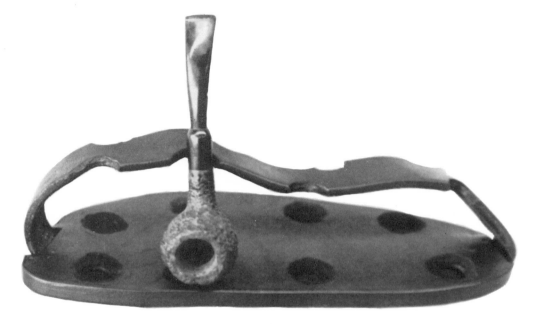

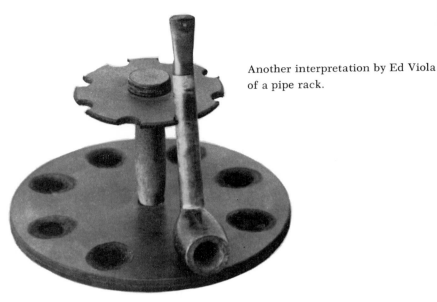

Another interpretation by Ed Viola of a pipe rack.

RIVETS

Rivets are also permanent fasteners. They are used to attach parts such as straps, or to hold parts in a fold of leather such as buckles on a belt or strap, or to strengthen stress points in seams or pockets. Rivets can be ornamental and do come in various metal colors, designs, and sizes.

Rivets usually come in two parts, one with a head and an internal shaft and another that fits over it with a cap and an external shaft. The shaft part becomes buried in the thickness of the leather, leaving both caps showing. To attach a rivet, ready the proper sized hole to accommodate both parts of the shaft, place the inner rivet section on a metal plate, string the leather onto it; place the cap part over this on the grain side of the leather and pound these parts together with a sharp blow from a metal hammer. They will be permanently affixed. These rivets come with shafts approximately ¾, ⅜, ½, and ⅝ inch long with heads or caps to match in proportion. There are tools with concave heads that press the caps together so that no hammer marks are made on the rivet cap.

A split rivet has a cap and shaft with a split in it like an old-fashioned clothespin. To attach a split rivet, make an appropriate sized hole, insert the rivet, and then bend the top prongs outward in opposite directions manually or by wedging a tool in the splits. Keep the split part concealed on the wrong side or underside of your design.

EYELETS AND GROMMETS

Eyelets and grommets differ in size. Eyelets are smaller; grommets are wider and flatter. Both are shallow tubes ending up with rings at both ends and are used to reinforce circular openings as for laces and straps. They are available in a wide variety of sizes, metals, colors, and patterns. Eyelet openings begin at about ¼ inch diameter. An eyelet is a one-piece finding—a tube with a collarlike flange on one end. A grommet is a two-piece finding, a collarlike flange on a tube for one part and a separate ring for the other. An eyelet setter is used to attach the eyelet. It bends part of the tube's lip over the leather. Grommets are set with grommet setters, bending part of the tube over the second ring.

To set an eyelet or grommet, form an appropriate sized hole to accommodate the shaft. Push the tube of the eyelet or grommet through the opening. Then place the eyelet and leather on a solid, hard base; place the eyelet setter on top in the open end and tap it gently with a hammer so the eyelet metal spreads open and forms a collar or lip around the leather. Use the same procedure for the grommet, except place the ring over the shaft so it sits on the leather. For each size grommet, there is a corresponding tool setter and anvil.

Some eyelet setters look like paper punches and can be used in the same tool that sets snaps.

SNAPS

Snaps are temporary closings that permit opening and closing and are used on wallet flaps, pocketbooks, belts, etc., and as clothing fasteners. They are available in a wide variety of colors, metals, sizes, patterns, and shapes. When selecting a snap, make certain that you buy a quality product. Snaps take a great

deal of wear and tear. Also when placing
snaps on thin leather, add a reinforcing
piece.

   Snaps come in four parts, two for the
top and two for the bottom. For each size
snap there is a corresponding setter. Each
setter is equipped with its own instructions.
Snaps do not usually require premade holes
in the leather for installation. There is usually
a hidden prong system that holds snaps in
place.

MAKING A WALLET

   The pattern is traced onto the leather.

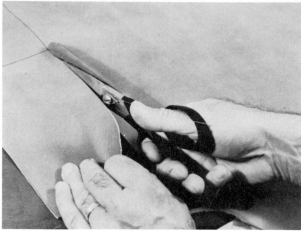

Using a leather shears, the leather is cut
out.

The piece is batiked as shown in the section on batiking. Then with dividers a
stitching line is marked along the edges to
contain stitches.

A spacing wheel is used to indicate where stitching holes should be.

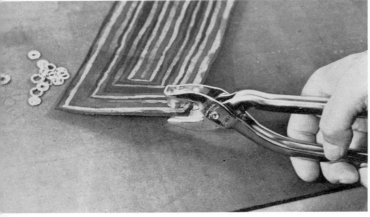

Snaps need to be attached before stitching the leather into a form. The top section is mechanically pressed into place with a special die.

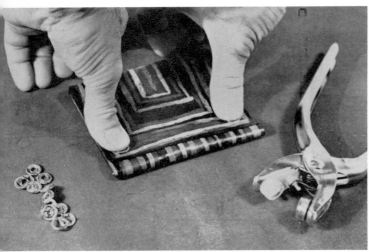

The top snap is pressed over the bottom to indicate where the bottom snaps should be attached.

Dies are changed and the bottom sections of the snaps are placed into the top and bottom sections of the tool.

The snaps then are pressed into place.

This wallet is made of two pieces of leather to form extra pockets when one section is creased and folded. A lockstitch awl is used with black waxed thread to sew parts together. Here the awl's needle, which contains thread from an enclosed bobbin, is pierced through the leather and a free length of the same thread is threaded through a loop made by the needle.

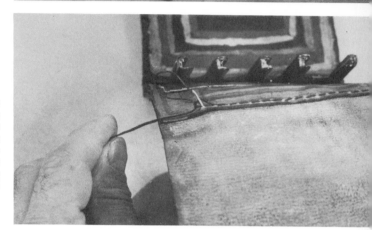

When the awl is withdrawn, the stitch is locked.

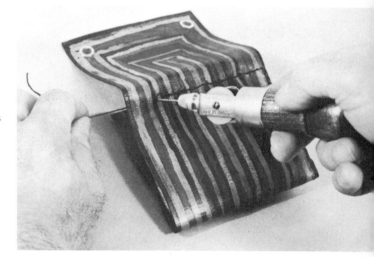

Stitches and edges are hammered to smooth out any unevenness.

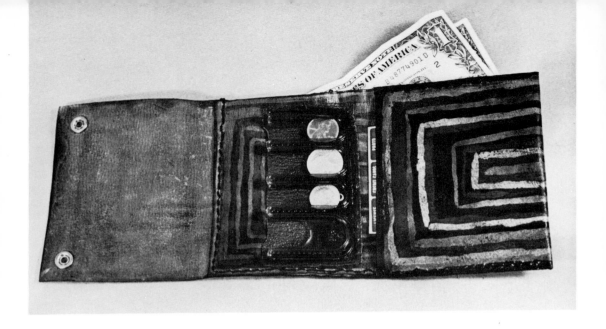

The completed wallet.

An assortment of Walter Dyer wallets.

The capacious interior of a Walter Dyer wallet. Note the use of a hand-stitched running stitch using beeswaxed thread.

ZIPPERS

The installation of zippers is described in chapter 9 on Clothing, even though zippers are used in wallets, notebooks, and briefcases.

BUCKLES

Buckles are fastening devices that require straps of various sizes to hold them in place. Buckles are attached with a strap and this strap is held in place with rivets, snaps, or by hand sewing. A second strap of varied length, depending on the item, is threaded through the buckle, thereby effecting a temporary closing. Sometimes the strap that is threaded through the buckle is also strung through a keeper that holds it in place. This may be a metal or leather strip around the strap and functions to keep the strap from flapping.

RINGS, LOOPS, AND DEES

These findings are intermediary attachments acting as flexible links between straps, belts, laces, and the body of the item. Rings, loops, and dees are usually metal and come in all colors and various sizes. They are attached with straps of various widths and lengths. And their straps, in turn, are attached to the background with rivets or by hand sewing.

Rings, loops, and dees differ in their configurations. Rings are circles, dees are shaped like a "D," and loops are other than circles and dees, usually with various contours ranging from rectangles to shapes like drawer pulls.

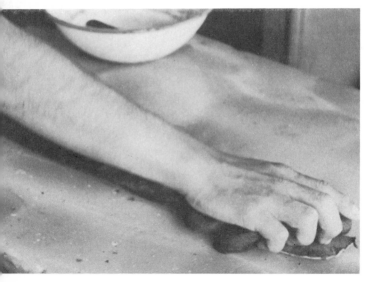

LEATHER AS BELT AND LINING

A piece of old dyed leather found its way into a belt in the studio of Justo Santa Anna Mancera, Oaxaca, Mexico.

The leather strip is being reclaimed by dampening it with a sponge and water.

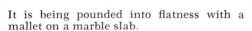
It is being pounded into flatness with a mallet on a marble slab.

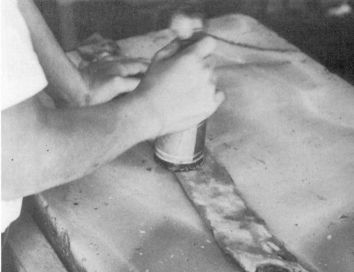

Excess is skived off in a skiving machine.

It is pounded into behaving once again.

Dividers are used to indicate width. Two parallel edges are assured. The woven belt from Santo Tomas in the foreground will be used as the outside.

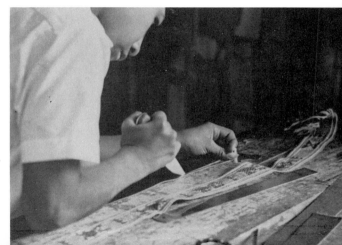

Excess is trimmed away.

Cement is spread over the cloth . . .

. . . and the skin side of the leather.

The cloth belt is carefully pressed onto the leather.

Where the belt is to narrow down, the cloth is pinched into a dart.

Excess is sliced away.

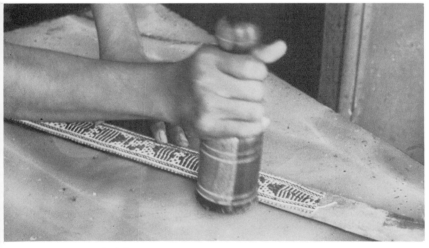

The piece is pounded flat.

A leather flap is measured and traced into the proper shape.

A mark indicates where it is to go. A similar piece is also prepared for the buckle end.

Cement is spread over both surfaces.

The piece is pressed and smoothed into place.

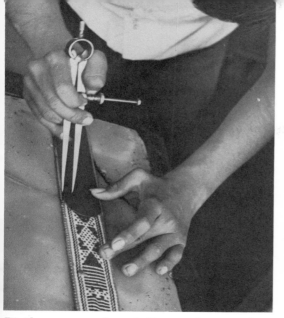

Dividers are used to indicate where machine stitching is to be used.

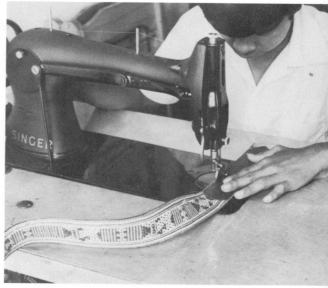

The flap is double-stitched around the edge.

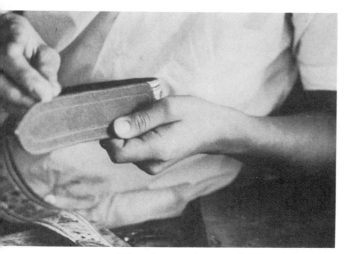

Edge dressing is spread around the edge.

The leather is rubbed with a hardwood slicker to smooth and compress it.

Dividers are used to indicate where belt holes will be punched.

Holes are punched. Grommets were added to the belt holes.

And holes are cut for the rivets to keep the buckle in place.

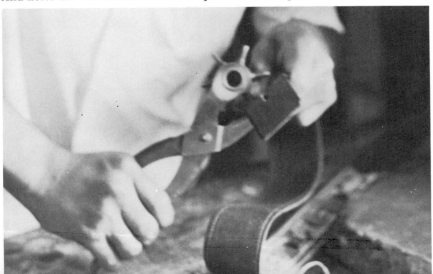

Edges are sealed again.

The buckle is put into place.

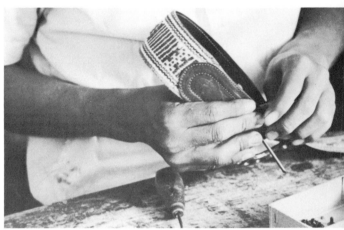

Rivets are inserted into the holes . . .

. . . and pounded closed.

A belt loop is being hand stitched.

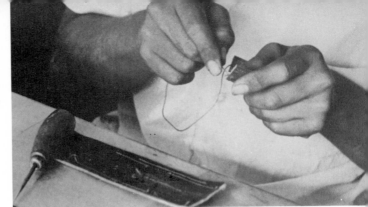

Then it is slid onto the belt.

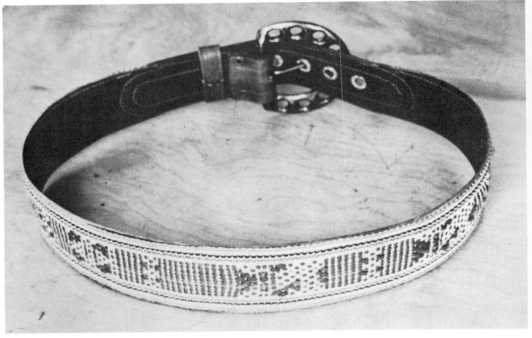

After all that, the completed belt sold for $3.50.

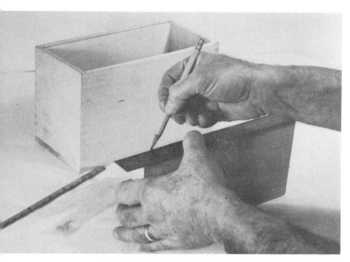

COVERING A BOX-POCKETBOOK

The box is measured in order to make a paper pattern. The pattern is fitted over the box to make certain of an exact fit.

The leather is cut around the pattern. Edges that will be overlapped are skived.

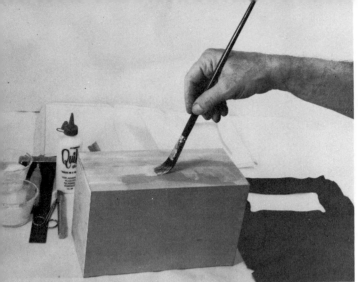

A flexible vinyl glue (Quik) is brushed on the box.

Suede leather is overlaid and a brayer is used to establish an airtight bond.

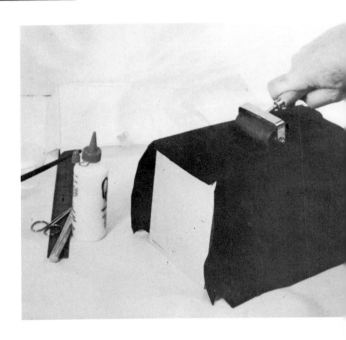

Leather is sliced around curved edges and in corners to assure a nonbulky fit and then glued into place. Sides and lid are covered the same way. Then hardware is attached.

The completed purse with a decoupage panel.

The same purse with another panel, opened to reveal the lid, its hardware, and the lining.

Justo Santa Anna Mancera tooled the leather design and covered the box that is next to it.

The interior section is covered with suede.

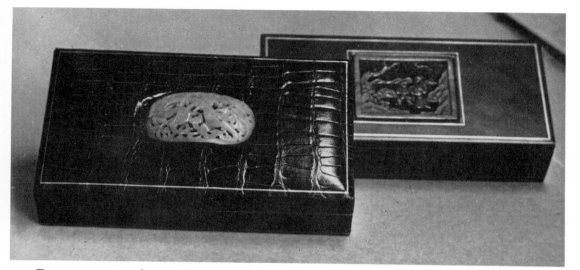

Two very precious boxes. The one on the left is alligator and sports a carved jade ornament. The one on the right is calf and has an orange soapstone carved scene. Made in the studios of the Foelich Leathercraft Co.

A Gallery of Ideas Showing Ways of Attaching Leather to Create Shapes

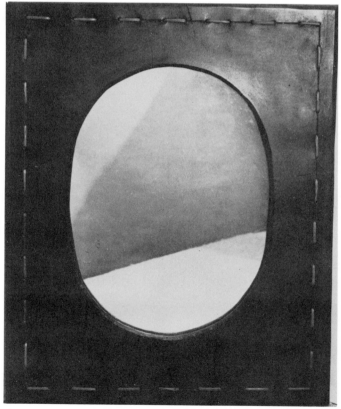

A running stitch with thread (and cement) was used to make this mirror. By Murry Kusmin.

Thonging in a cross-stitch design decorates and functions as a way to attach parts of this purse by Jeff Slaboden.

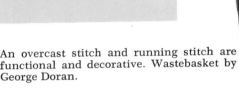

An overcast stitch and running stitch are functional and decorative. Wastebasket by George Doran.

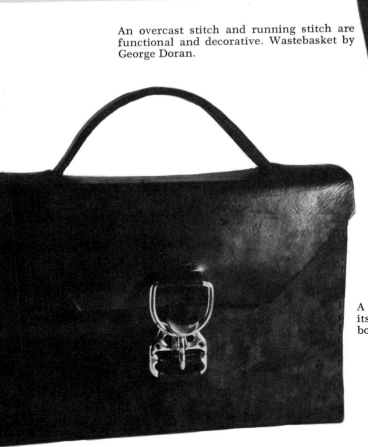

A running stitch, finer in proportion to its use, for this briefcase by Jeff Slaboden.

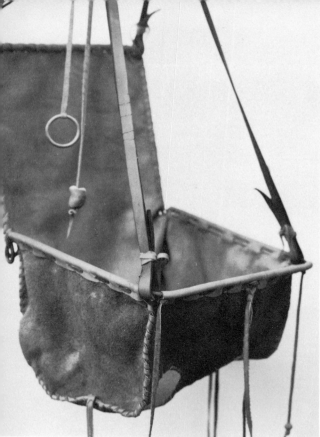

An overcast stitch and running stitch using thonging hold this baby swing together. By Renaissance Leather.

A lockstitch with a lockstitch awl was used along with reinforcing rivets. Pipe holder by Ted St. Germain.

Decorative and functional lockstitching. Belt by Ted St. Germain.

The lid of this box is held in place with cement and nails. The sides are crossstitched.

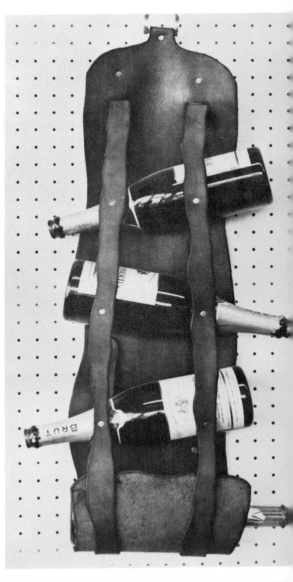

Three ways to store wine, each using leather straps and rivets to attach parts. This one is by Ed Viola.

Another wine rack, by Jeff Slaboden.

And a third version, by John Anderson.

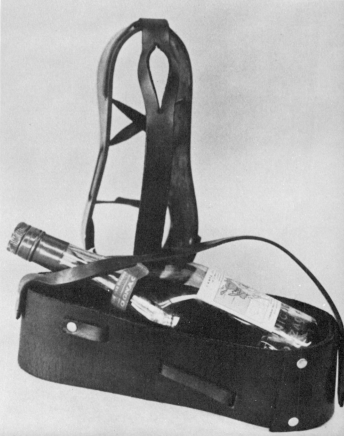

For a single bottle of that special vintage, a nest hooked up with rivets and straps. By Ed Viola.

A more traditional shape for a mirror is machine stitched around the edge. By Ed Viola.

Frames attached with cobbler nails using denting caused by ball peen hammer to create a te tured effect. By Ed Viola.

A shelf supported by rods strung through leather straps and attached to rings with rivets. By Jeff Slaboden.

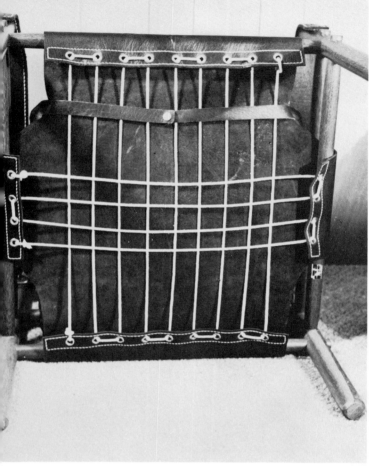

This leather chair based on the director-chair theme is held together with machine stitching, grommets, rivets, snaps, rope, and swiveling loops, as well as buckles for the backrest. Nothing is missing!

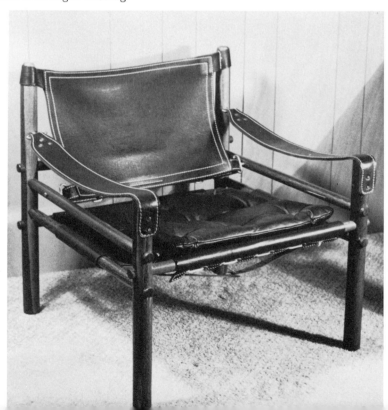

Machine stitching, grommets, rivets, buckles, and snaps hold the parts of this knapsack together. By Walter Dyer.

Tie-dyed suede.

A jerkin made from a McCall pattern with special pocket detailing in a cross-stitch.

Sculpture of formed leather by Lorne Peterson.

Raymond White's modeled and incised purse, trimmed and detailed with lacing.

Mary Fish's pocketbook of formed leather.

A mirror covered in brown suede with beige embroidery and fringing, by Florence Sohn and Ed Ghossn of L'Insolite.

"Fallen Bird" by Murry Kusmin, a tapestry of suede and belting strips suspended from driftwood.

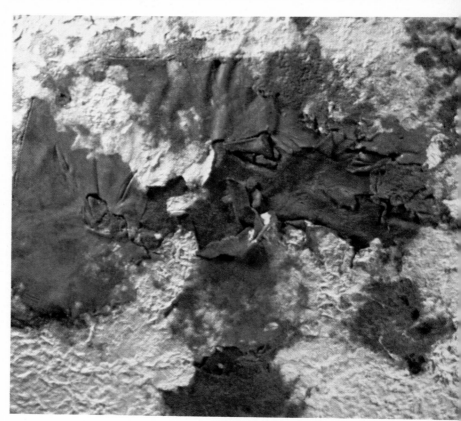

A "compage" of handmade paper and leather by Golda Lewis.

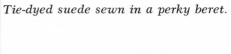

Tie-dyed suede sewn in a perky beret.

Leather fringes are trimmed with beads and strung on a four-plait leather "cord."

"Shield" by John Fargotstein in leather with fur and feather.

A few slices in a flat leather cir convert it into a candle sling.

Dyed and formed leather leaves are combined with branches made of leather machinery belting in "Autumn Leaves" by Murry Kusmin.

...ase in wet-formed leather and fur by John ...derquist. Note the function and emphasis ...the overcast stitching of each section.

This Fulani, or Maure, saddlebag from Africa is a relative of the Moroccan Shikara, a traditional bag carried by men. It is leather appliqué with leather embroidery.

The tradition of this Moroccan leather embroidered wallet stems back centuries in time. The skill is practiced today as it was in yesteryear.

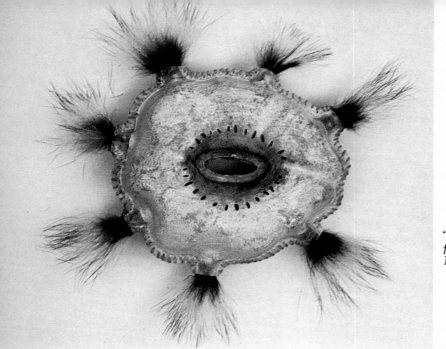

"Rawhide Fetish Rattle" in formed rawhide and fur by Nancy Flanagan.

A reverse appliqué design, detailed with a hand running stitch by Ben Liberty.

Rosettes of beads are sewn to a leather base for this necklace.

Pocketbook with a burned design by Yael-Lurie and construction by Jean Pierre Larochette. The black dye is asphaltum.

Leather strips are used to embroider this pouch bag from northern Nigeria, West Africa.

An embroidered and suede covered bench with un-attached cushions by L'Insolite is a luxury to look at as well as to sit on.

This Taureg wallet from Timbuktu, Mali, is in two pieces. The top slides down a woven "cord" fitting like an envelope over the compartments of the wallet. The design is made by slicing and then peeling thin slivers of the top surface of the leather.

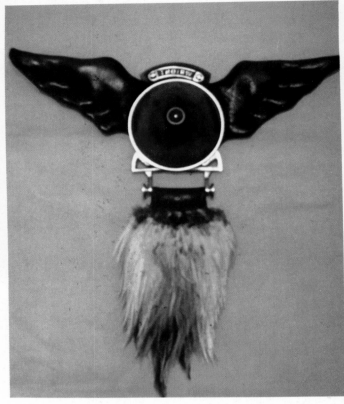

A Dean Massey and Fred Williams sculpture.

Two fans from northern Nigeria. The top one opens to form a circular pleated fan. The bottom one, trimmed in leather, has the cowhide hairs intact. The entire construction of both fans is entirely of leather.

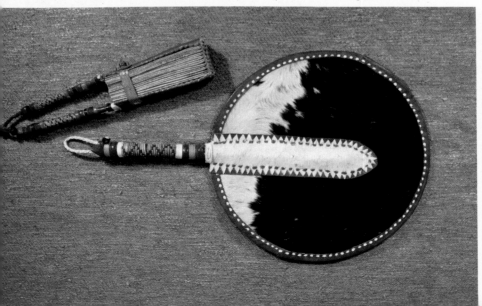

5

Leather Finishing: Exotic Coloring, Tooling, and Burning

LEATHER DECORATING: A POINT OF VIEW

There are many ways of changing the surface appearance of a piece of leather. Some add color and pattern, others carve, incise, and raise areas; another group of techniques employs various kinds of embellishments such as rivets, beads, yarns. Some of these approaches produce effective and striking results. But among all these techniques we do find atrocious examples that completely mutilate the leather. Granted that sometimes leather becomes a vehicle to exhibit a communication, much as a piece of canvas or wood; most useful forms, however, exist for the sake of their own functions, an existence made possible by the very properties and virtues of leather. The abiding question is: How far should we go to change the initial character of leather or to obscure its surface qualities?

Consider these good design characteristics:

Design is an expression of its material. Is leather made to imitate another material? Is the design better suited for another material?

Design of each part is consistent with the overall intent and effect. Does the color, pattern, texture of the decoration detract from or relate to the whole effect?

Fashion and style changes fluctuate and become trend setting. One day carving is the mode, another dyed patterns, still at different intervals the preference is for pure, unembellished surfaces. Within all these variations there is the potential for excellence or for a poverty of taste. It is a matter of exposure to good design and the development of a design philosophy. This is not easy to come by. It requires openness and experience.

COLORING MATERIALS

Tie dye, batik, block printing, and marking pens are some of the many ways that leather can be colored with pattern. There are many more mechanical ways such as the use of brushes, sponges, and stencils to achieve effects.

Acrylic paints, chemicals that stain, household dyes, batik and tie dyes, indelible marking pens, and traditional dyes such as aniline that are water- or alcohol-based are some coloring materials.

Leather is unpredictable, inasmuch as tannery processes and unique characteristics of a particular skin such as porosity and texture can greatly influence what happens to color and a technique. A design process may work very well on one piece of leather and fail on a similar piece. It pays to practice an idea on a scrap of leather before proceeding to a large decorating commitment.

An assortment of various powdered crystalline aniline dyes.

Basic preparations and methods of application for overall dyeing discussed in the previous chapter hold true here. The following materials for dyeing are variations of basic procedures.

Acrylic paints, if diluted with enough water to make them translucent, work well aesthetically, but when applied in full consistency (although acrylic most often effects a tenacious bond with the leather) do not permit the quality of leather to show through. One might as well use cardboard or canvas.

Almost any liquid will impart a color change on a leather surface—coffee, beet juice, tea, onion, even water. But there are also chemicals that can provide just the color effect you are looking for.

To use the following chemicals, start with a 3 percent solution and add three or four drops of this 3 percent solution to a cup of water. Apply it with a cotton swab or sponge. If the color is not intense enough, add a few more drops.

Bichromate of Potash: colors leather brown and is irreversible (cannot be removed).

Potassium Hydroxide: colors leather brown. Too much will "burn" the leather. A 3 percent oxalic acid solution can bleach the effect.

Permanganate of Potash: produces a brown or gray effect, depending on the strength of the solution and the kind of leather. It tends to streak.

Sulfate of Iron: Colors leather a pale gray to a very deep blue-gray. Too much tends to harden and crack the leather. Bleaching with the oxalic acid solution can reduce overcoloring somewhat.

Sulfate of iron over *potassium hydroxide* colors leather a deep black.

Picric acid: turns leather to a pale yellow. Over *sulfate of iron*, the effect will be a green. Various shades of green can be achieved using different combinations of these two ingredients and water.

Household dyes and special batik and tie dyes also color leather effectively. Just follow directions on the package. Remember that when water is applied to vegetable-tanned leather it tends to cause some stiffening. You can recondition your leather by rubbing it with saddle soap, neat's-foot oil, Vaseline, or Lexol after dyeing has dried, of course, unless the leather is suede.

Aniline dyes of various types work well, even those formulated for wood. Colors show up on unglazed, unfinished vegetable-tanned, uncolored leathers. Colors also are specifically made for leather and sold under proprietary labels such as Fiebing's and Omega.

Fiebing's and Omega have a wide selection of colors. For those who use dyes in large quantities, it is best to buy dry colors in powder form and mix the dye with the suggested water, alcohol (Synosol), or mineral oil and spirit solvent.

Both sides of the leather can be dyed. If you wet the skin first, dyes penetrate deeper and more intense color results; on dry leather, when the pores are tighter, dyes will not be received in the same quantity, producing lighter, softer colors.

When dyeing, start with lighter, overall colors. As dyeing progresses, colors can be darker and applied with daubers, cotton swabs, pipe cleaners, or brushes.

SPECIAL CONSIDERATIONS OF COLOR MIXING

Colors mix easily and build up as colors are overlaid. It is best to begin with a light value, neutral hue leather that has a clean surface. (See use of oxalic acid solution for cleaning in previous chapter.) For water soluble dyes, it is best to use a brush because

Use one teaspoon of oxalic acid to one pint of warm water and stir until dissolved.

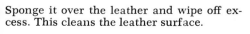

Sponge it over the leather and wipe off excess. This cleans the leather surface.

cotton or lamb's-wool applicators hold back color solids. When using mineral oil and spirit solvent dyes, saturate your applicator in mineral oil first, unless you want your dye to streak and give a grainy effect. A mineral oil saturated applicator smooths the dye on more evenly because dye is sucked into the fibers of the applicator more evenly. The first stroke, therefore, will be as even as the fifth stroke.

CROSS-DYEING

Cross-dyeing involves mixing of colors directly on the leather, instead of premixing color in a bottle. A more uniform and intense color results. Colors can be built in the following combinations:

Red over *blue* makes *purple*.
Yellow over *red* makes a *brighter red* (scarlet).
Yellows tend to lighten and brighten colors.
Yellow over *magenta* makes *red*.
Yellow over *blue-violet* makes *green*.
Green over *dark violet* makes *dark blue*.
Intense blue over *orange* makes *brown*.
Green over *bright red* makes *brown-black*.
Green over *brown* makes *black*.
Green over *purple* makes *black*.
Green over *orange* makes *olive green*.

Browns can vary from tans, when yellows are overlaid, to variations of warmth and coolness when orange, red, or purple is added. It is best to build to *black* in two or more steps.

Any transparent color, whether aniline, acrylic, batik, household dyes, India inks, or marking pens, will mix more or less intensely following the above chart.

BLACKS AND THEIR SPECIAL PROBLEMS

Blacks often rub off on hands and clothing. Because it is difficult to obtain opaque, deep blacks, it is best to build up blacks through several steps. One excellent way is to dye the leather blue, green, or dark brown using spirit solvent dyes because they are more intense. Then apply black lightly the first time. When dry, rub the surface with a flannel cloth. Then apply a more liberal coating of black a second time. Let it dry thoroughly. Then with a damp cloth, buff the surface to remove excess black particles and follow this with a buffing with a flannel cloth. A final coating of neat's-foot oil should be used to help mature the color and keep the leather from cracking. Spirit solvent dyes tend to dry the leather.

A technique used in Mexico is to dilute asphaltum with benzine (gasoline) until it is of a paintable consistency and to brush this on the leather. After the asphaltum dries thoroughly, in about twenty-four hours, buff, and then apply a wax coating.

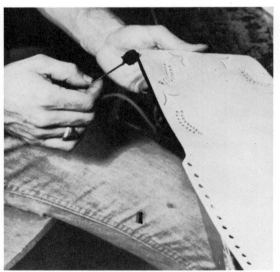

Edge coating (or enameling) can be accomplished with a dauber as shown here, or with a cotton swab, pipe cleaner, or paintbrush.

Dye does not take too readily on the flesh side as seen here, and is streaky when applied with a sponge.

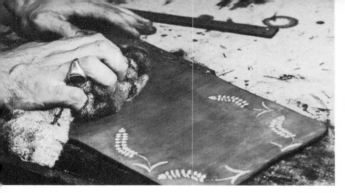

Application of color is more even when applied with a Turkish towel and is more intense on the grain side.

Texturing is possible when a darker color is used very sparingly with a large, stiff brush.

ANTIQUING

Antiquing colors come in solid and liquid formulas and in a water vehicle. To apply, whatever antiquing you use, overlay a generous amount and then wipe away surplus color. Antiquing is applied *after* the base color has dried.

LEATHER ENAMELS AND LACQUER

These colors fall into the same category as acrylic. They are paints. Whereas lacquers can be transparent, enamels obscure the surface quality of the leather. Lacquers have a glossy effect producing their own surface. Clear lacquer or shellac can be used over a particular area to retain the original color of the leather, while the rest of the leather is colored with dyes or antiquing. It acts as a resist.

Bright clear colors are hand painted with transparent lacquers on shallow machine-embossed figures on this eyeglass case from India. Note the Florentine style of lacing.

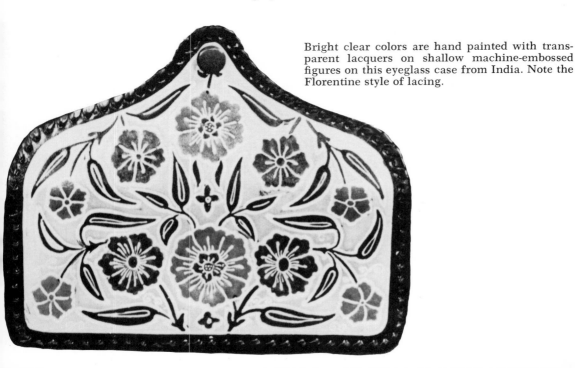

Jeff Slaboden's cabinet doors are colored with aniline dyes; the figures, with acrylic paint. Neat's-foot oil was used on the leather doors as a preservative.

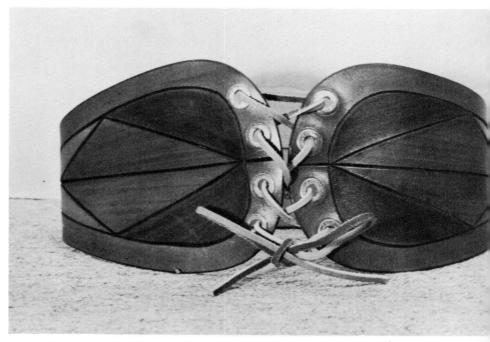

Murry Kusmin used different colors of aniline dyes to color areas circumscribed by incised areas of this belt. Incisions were dyed a darker color as are the edges of this belt.

Lacquers also are used on this Maure, or Fulbe (African), pillow cover. Black lines are finely drawn.

TIE DYE

Tie dye can be accomplished on leathers that are soft and light enough to be folded, on chrome-tanned suedes, and particularly on light valued, neutral backgrounds.

Prepare your leather by wiping it with a soft cloth to remove oils and grease or with the oxalic acid solution. Different effects are obtained by folding and bending or wrapping the leather in different patterns. Prepare your dye in a container deep enough to receive the areas you are tying. Use either wax-coated string or rubber bands to bind the areas. Crinkle or fold a small area at a time. Folding can be accomplished in many different ways for a variety of effects. Then wrap that

section tightly at intervals with your string or rubber bands. Insert it in the prepared dye. Allow the piece to sit in the dye until the color intensity you wish has been achieved. Many factors are at play here—the color and type of dye you are using, the thickness and type of leather and the temperature of the room, the way you folded and wrapped the leather. Remove the piece, blot off excess, and while still wet remove the string or rubber bands. Flatten the leather out and allow it to dry on newspaper. If, finally, you need to press out wrinkles (this may not be necessary), use a medium-hot iron and press over brown kraft paper after the leather is completely dry. Too much heat will hasten the deterioration of leather.

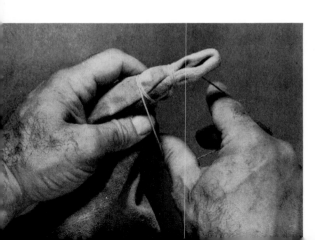

TIE DYE

Chrome-tanned suede is folded and then wrapped tightly into a pattern with a rubber band.

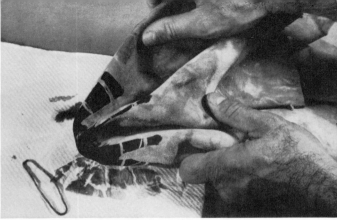

Rinse off excess dye under cold running water and remove the rubber band while the leather is still wet.

Hazel's Batik Dye, Fibrec, Dylon, Rit, or Tintex is mixed in the recommended proportion with cold or warm water. Usually the proportion is three to six tablespoons to two gallons of water. The addition of salt, or fixer, usually is required for cold water dyes. When the dye mixture is ready, dip the tied area into the dye and permit it to remain there until the color depth you wish has been achieved—usually from two to thirty minutes.

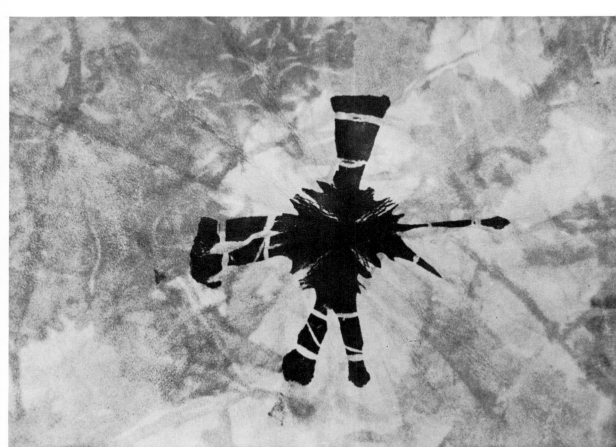

Spread out the leather, flat, on absorbent paper toweling and allow to dry.

An example of tie-dye suede in subtle variations of blues, turquoise, and a touch of light red-violets. Created by Sirois Leather, Inc., tanners.

BATIK

Batik probably originated in the Far East and is still practiced there today. It is essentially a wax resist method of dyeing. Wherever wax is placed, dye will not penetrate. So wax is added to the leather in an appropriate pattern and dye is painted over the entire piece. Whatever is waxed will retain the original color of the leather.

When the dye is dry, the next wax design is painted or stamped on that first color to preserve it. And the process continues from light colored dyes to the darkest color. Each time succeeding colors mix over the previous color, e.g., blue over yellow results in green. If you do not want a mixture of color, then, after the initial waxing, paint on dyes in patterns of color and then proceed waxing and dyeing. You increase your color range this way.

To remove the wax press the leather under a thick layer of newspaper with a medium-hot iron until the wax melts off and is absorbed into the newspaper. Where the first wax was placed you may find a slightly raised surface and some puckering of edges might result. This doesn't happen on all leather. Make certain that you do not overheat the leather with your iron.

BATIK

Melt wax safely in a wax melter as shown here, in an electric frying pan, or in the top section of a double boiler. I used three parts paraffin to one part beeswax.

On a clean piece of leather, paint areas you wish to preserve with wax.

Apply a generous amount of water-based dye (alcohol-based dyes will dissolve the wax) in your lightest shade first.

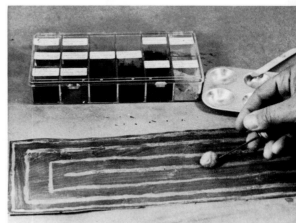

When this has dried, paint areas you want to preserve this last color with wax. Then repeat the dyeing and coloring process by using your next darkest color, considering that the color will cross dye with the color you applied earlier. (For what happens to cross-dyed colors, refer to the list in this chapter.)

After the waxing-dyeing procedure is completed, press the leather between absorbent paper with a medium-warm iron to melt away (and absorb) the wax. The final piece was shown earlier when it was made into a wallet.

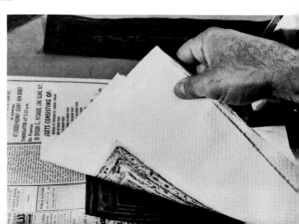

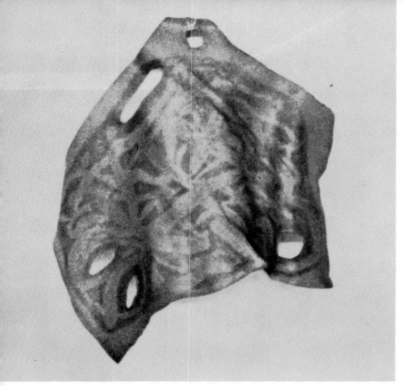

A sculpture hanging by Genevieve Barnett using a batik decoration. *Courtesy Genevieve Barnett*

A mask by Genevieve Barnett again employing batik as her decorating agent. *Courtesy Genevieve Barnett*

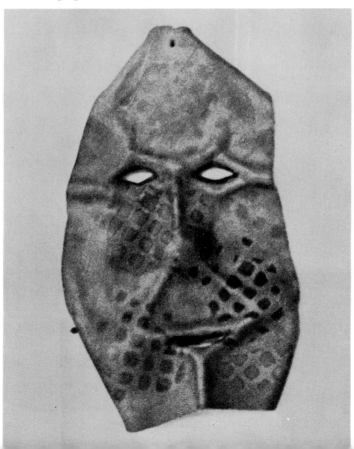

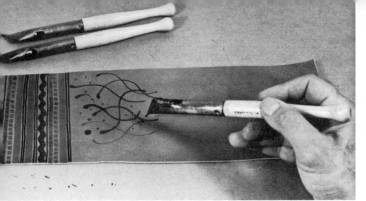

Another approach with batik is to apply wax with a tjanting, which is a small container for melted wax with a penlike spout. It has been used by Indonesians for centuries to apply fine lines of wax to cloth.

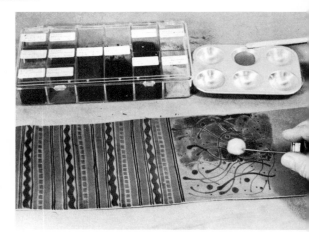

Coat the area with dye. In this case a dauber is used.

Again, when the dye is dry, apply wax. The brush covers broader areas.

Overlay your next darkest color and repeat these operations until the desired combinations of colors have been achieved.

Press the leather between absorbent paper with a warm iron to absorb the wax.

MARKING PENS

Indelible marking pens with felt tips are as new as batik is old. If colors are relatively colorfast, it is a direct and great way to add design to a surface. There is no special technique, except to draw directly onto clean leather. Of course, as with all decorating techniques, the entire surface should be protected with a wax coating when you are finished.

MARKING PENS AS DYE

Indelible marking pens work beautifully. They should be the best quality you can get with colors that will not fade quickly. Just apply them in any creative way you know.

The design on this cape by the Girasol group (Guadalajara, Mexico) was created with marking pens.

Another design treatment using marking pens, also by the Girasol group.

A detail of the skirt design.

BLOCK PRINTING

Almost anything can be used to transfer dye to the leather surface—a linoleum block, a carved piece of wood, a carved rubber eraser, scrap materials, a pencil eraser. Almost anything that has a flat surface, that will accept dye when pressed onto the leather surface, will permit the transfer of dye to the leather, has potential. Repeat patterns or larger single units can be carried out this way. Dyes vary according to the kind of material your transfer block is made of. Water-based dyes will bead on some surfaces, whereas alcohol, mineral oil, and spirit solvent dyes will hold onto most surfaces.

It is a good idea to control the amount of dye that you are delivering to the leather surface with your printing "block." One way to limit color is to make a padding with tissues or paper toweling and place it in an aluminum-foil pan. Add your dye to the paper and then press your "block" onto the paper pad to pick up color. You can also use a sponge as a pad for ink. Printing is direct, using hand pressure, one unit at a time, onto the leather. Various repeat patterns are possible. Overlapping of shapes and variations of color expand possibilities even further. Overlapping and repeating simple geometric elements almost guarantee a successful result.

Mix dyes together into a heavier pastelike consistency. Fibrec has a thickener for its dye colors.

Prepare your block or piece you are going to print with. This is a gum eraser that is being cut into two different sizes of triangles.

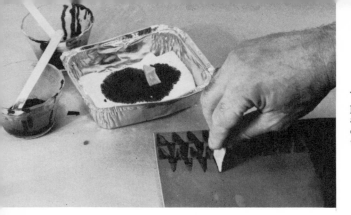

You can dip your block directly into the dye, paint color on the block, or make a stamp pad of absorbent paper in an aluminum dish. Place color on your block in some way and immediately transfer it to the leather with an even pressure.

Two colors and two shapes are overlapped to achieve a third color and shape while still permitting the natural color of the leather to show through, uniting all the design elements.

The finished piece is being waxed to preserve the color and surface, and to recondition the leather.

The completed sample. The batik area puckered because the wax was hot and caused swelling into an embossed look (that also caused puckering). A heavier leather would not pucker.

TOOLING

Tooling is an overall term that encompasses the mechanical manipulation of leather to create permanent depressions and raised areas resulting in a design. This can be done by stamping leather with various kinds of dies, carving leather with a knife to cut into and raise portions, incising by lifting out thin slivers of leather, embossing, or repoussé, by modeling the leather with handtool pressure on the grain and/or flesh side.

Tooling has a tradition of ugliness, especially as it was expressed in Western-style designs using flowers or animals in poorly organized embellishments. But there have been very handsome designs produced with these techniques. Some old Spanish carved and incised designs are very handsome. Con-

temporary craftsmen also have come up with refreshing interpretations.

Tooling is done on "tooling" leather, that is, full-grained vegetable-tanned (oak, preferably) firm calfskin, steerhide, cowhide, or strap leather of uniform thickness.

All tooling requires the leather to be moistened to create *cased leather* (moist leather). First, apply water with a light spray or damp sponge over the flesh side, then apply it lightly to the grain surface until the color darkens uniformly. Let the leather stand until the moisture is distributed and the surface begins to dry slightly. The cased leather is then ready for tooling. If the leather is too moist, depressions will swell back to a flatness. On the other hand, if the leather is too dry, the tool will be difficult to manipulate and could rip the leather or not make a very great impression. As you work, remoisten the

Fourteenth-century leatherwork in incising and repoussé, showing the scenes from the life of St. Margaret on this reliquary shoe. *Courtesy The Metropolitan Museum of Art*

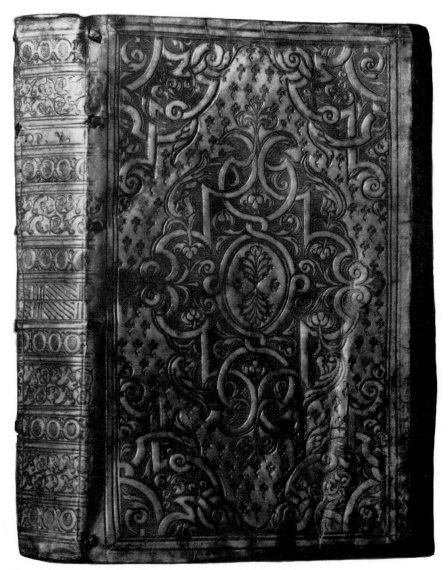

Plutarch's *Les Oeuvres* deserved an elegant binding in 1574. This is tooling on a limp vellum. *Courtesy The Metropolitan Museum of Art, Bequest of Mrs. Mary Strong Shattuck, 1935*

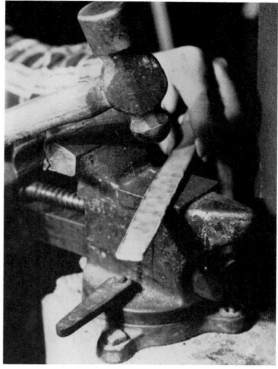

A ball peen hammer can bang texture into leather.

A sixteenth-century knife case in an incised and stamped design. *Courtesy The Metropolitan Museum of Art, Rogers Fund, 1951*

Carving into leather with a wood-cutting tool created this effect. Mirror by Ed Viola.

leather to maintain pliability. Use rust-proof tools in order to avoid rust stains. Permit the leather to dry completely before continuing on to other operations.

TRANSFER OF DESIGN

Designs can be transferred from thin paper by going over the entire design with a stylus or with a rounded metal tip of some kind such as an inkless ball-point pen. If the design is faint when you remove the paper, repeat the operation directly on the leather. This outlining type of design could suffice as a technique by pressing the lines again and making them more distinct. Edges can be rounded off with the pressure of a curved tool shaped like a nutpick. This approaches modeling.

MODELING

The more you depress areas around and within your outlines, the more other areas will stand out in relief. Moving the tool slowly back and forth over the leather compresses it.

EMBOSSING, OR REPOUSSÉ

After modeling one side you should see some indication of a pattern on the flesh side. If you cannot, then your leather is too thick

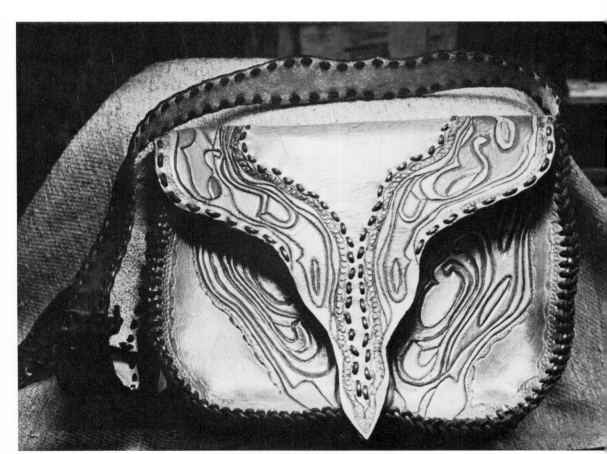

Modeled pocketbook by Raymond White.

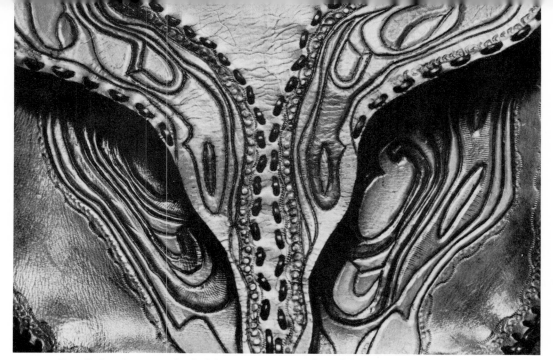

Detail showing use of stitching, stamping, and modeling to create the design.

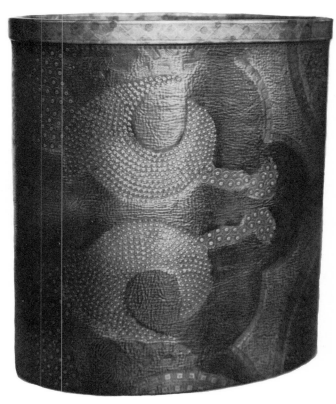

An embossed leather wastepaper basket by Foelich Leather Co.

A dice cup in a machine-embossed design.

for embossing. Place your leather grain side down on a piece of foam rubber, and with rotary and back and forth small movements press out the reverse side. This stretches the leather and more greatly accentuates the design. You can continue depressing and stretching on both sides.

When the leather has dried, reinforce your design by filling it with RTV silicone sealer or newspaper scraps saturated with rubber cement. A lining would probably be necessary to hide the unsightly filler.

STAMPING

Modeling, embossing, and any other technique could be combined with any other such as stamping.

Stamping requires the use of metal dies of some kind. Nail points and nailheads can work. Dies of any number of configurations and textures can be purchased separately or in sets.

To stamp a die, always on the grain side, hold the stamp vertically and strike the stamp with a mallet or hardwood plank. Practice on a scrap, so as to determine the amount of pressure you need without ripping the surface and yet achieving the amount of definition that you need.

Stamping dies require repeated operations; pressure should be consistent.

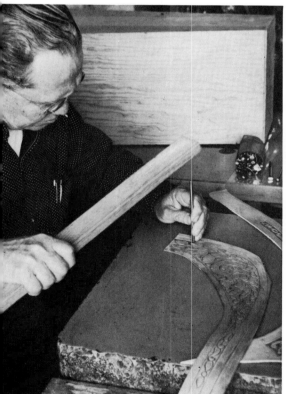

Details within the figures pressed and rubbed to create a modeled effect.

Justo Santa Anna Mancera pounds his die with an oak plank. He achieves a continuous modeling by dragging his tool along the water-dampened areas he is filling in with a background texture.

Some dies used to create a Mexican saddle design.

After carving, stamping, and coloring, edges are trimmed. Areas of the leather are then wet so that they can be cured and formed around a wooden base.

Parts of a saddle ready for assembly.

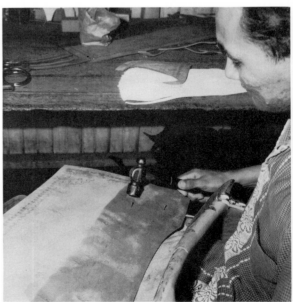

The leather is being attached to the wood with nails.

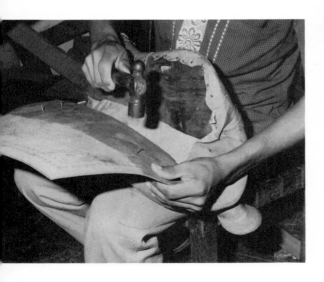

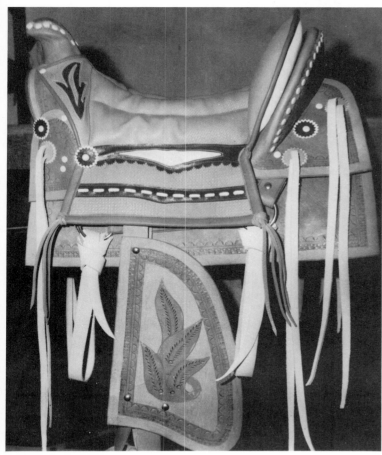

A completed saddle.

Another saddle showing appliqué, coloring, and stamping.

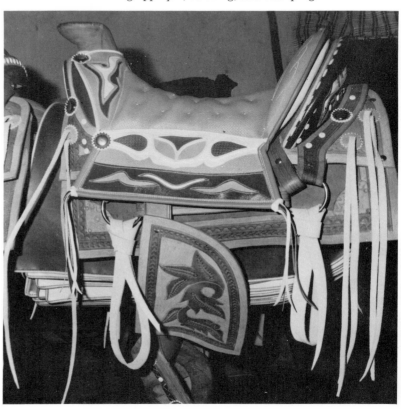

CARVING AND INCISING

Carving and incising are more difficult. The carving operation usually starts with an outline. A knife cuts around areas partway into the grain surface. A modeling tool or stamping die is used to depress areas around the incision. Some carving in the past involved cutting pockets or slits parallel with the grain and under the design, stuffing that area with a filler, then gluing and depressing edges. An embossed effect was observable, then, only on the grain side.

Incising cuts away slivers of leather in a bevel effect, usually with a very sharp swivel knife. The knife is held with the index finger depressing the yoke, and the thumb, middle, or fourth finger gripping the barrel. The little finger acts as a guide as you draw the knife along your outline. It takes practice to learn how to control this knife.

JOHN GIORDANO MAKING A STAMPED BELT

Tools are arrayed.

A latigo (yellow) belting length (seven to eight ounce) is edge beveled (#3), and a tip is cut on one end of the belt.

The buckle end is machine skived.

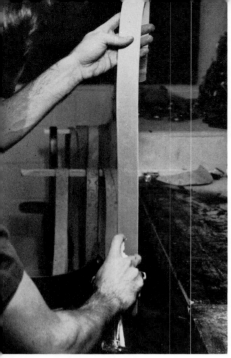

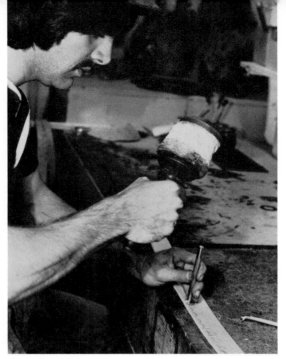

e belt is dampened with a spray of water
ready it for stamping.

John pounds away at a die to create a repeat design deep enough to keep overall dye color from
seeping into those units of the design. Tooling
along the edge seems to bend the leather into a
contour form.

Fiebling's alcohol dye (in black) is carefully painted in the tooled areas. The die
spreads within the tooling through capil-
lary action.

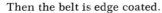

Then the belt is edge coated.

Using a felt-wrapped wooden block, John Giordano adds brown alcohol-based (ortho-dichlorobenzine) antiquing with a dauber.

He applies a small amount at a time so it doesn't seep into the tooling . . .

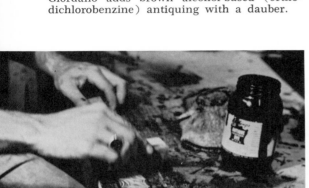

. . . and repeats the operation until the desired intensity is achieved.

A Turkish towel is handy to wipe away excess. No dye seeped into the yellow latigo tooled areas.

Snap holes are stamped on the buckle end.

Buckle holes are added on the flap end.

John Giordano's carved belt.

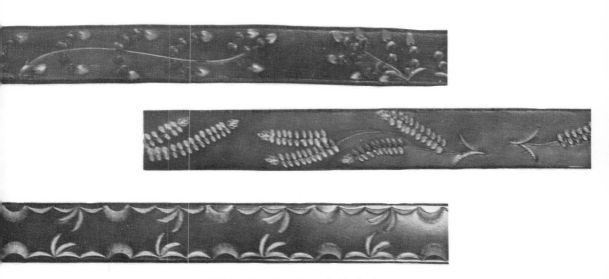

Some of John Giordano's tooled belt designs.

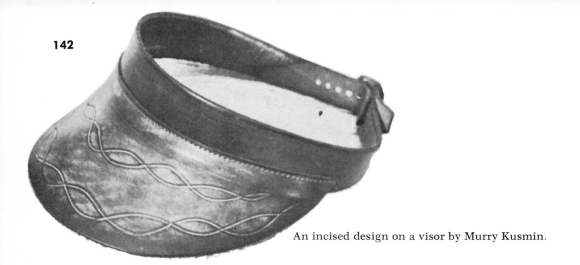

An incised design on a visor by Murry Kusmin.

Incised work on a canteen by Doug Shaffernoth.

A turtle, carved, incised, and modeled by Genevieve Barnett. *Courtesy Genevieve Barnett*

BURNING

Burning is like branding a hide. Instead of a red hot branding iron, an electrically controlled pencil is used. What it does is brown whatever area it touches. There is no smoking because the heat is not great enough to ignite the leather. The pencil is drawn slowly in a linear movement over the leather's (grain, suede, or split) surface. The result is a permanent brown line that can become a very attractive drawing or pattern.

Yael-Lurie Larochette drawing one of her imaginative designs (without recourse to any sketch), using an electric pencil.

A detail of her drawing (on dry leather, of course).

Her husband, Jean Pierre Larochette, paints areas with dyes.

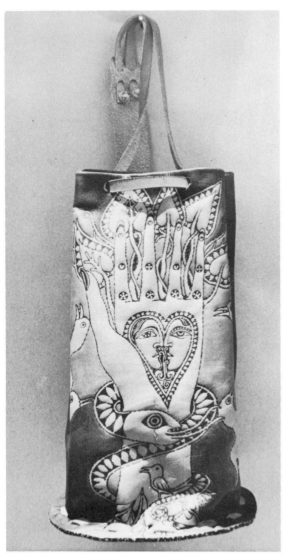

A pouch by Yael-Lurie and Jean Pierre Larochette.

Another by the same team.

Another style with a braided strap.

A witty wall hanging by Yael-Lurie. Note the use of rivets and straps for the hanging.

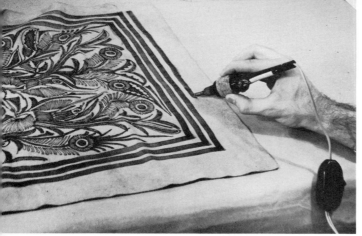

Another type of electric pencil commonly sold in hobby shops as a wood-burning tool is usable. Different points are available.

This design, Mexican in origin, is on split cowhide.

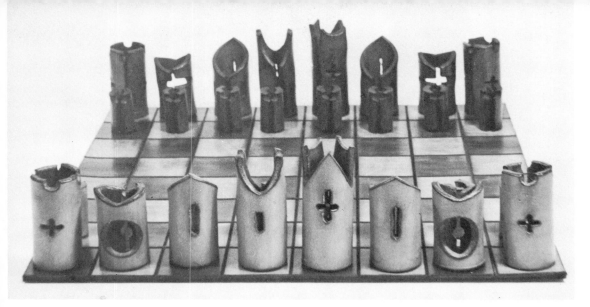

John Anderson's chess set with edges sporting a "burned" look.

LEATHER FINISHES

Finishes for leather are the final protective coats, often applied before or after parts are assembled. Most are commercially prepared. Only suede and splits do not need finishing because all the finishing is completed in the factory. Finish that penetrates deep into its fibers protects color from fading and resists staining from dirt or chemicals. Finishes fall into several categories: saddle soaps and cleaners, conditioners, waterproofing agents, and polishes. These are either pastes or liquids of varying viscosities.

SADDLE SOAPS AND CLEANERS

Saddle soap performs a dual service: it cleans and conditions the leather at the same time. It is applied with a wet sponge or brush, lathering it into the surface. Excess is wiped away with a dry cloth. The leather is buffed to a soft luster. Lexol, a liquid, is a soft saddle soap.

CONDITIONERS

Conditioners soften and revitalize non-sueded leathers, while leaving a soft surface luster. Some slight darkening may result. Most conditioners are applied with cloth, fingers, or brush, allowed to dry, and then polished with a soft cloth or flannel. Several thin coats are generally better than one heavy application. Vaseline makes an excellent dressing for leather bookbindings. After applying, let the bookbindings stand in a warm place for a few hours, and buff away excess with a soft cloth.

Conditioning replaces some of what is lost in decorating a surface. Lexol does the job here.

WATERPROOFING AGENTS

These liquids or pastes produce a water repellency and tend to soften leather. They are applied with fingers, cloth, brush, or sheep wool. A good waterproofing material is to mix one part neat's-foot oil with one part melted paraffin. Stir it thoroughly and apply it generously with your fingers.

Dubbin is an old term used to describe the process of dubbin onto leather, dubbin being an oil and tallow mixture used to preserve and waterproof leather, particularly boots.

POLISHES

The best polishes are those that require a final buffing to achieve a shine. Everybody knows how to use polish. Castor oil, surprisingly, makes a fine polish, if you can stand the odor. Rub it well into the leather. Let the oil "dry," and then buff with a soft cloth.

CLEANING AND CARING FOR LEATHERS

Saddle soaps and other leather conditioners help to clean smooth-grained surfaces.

Chrome-tanned leather can be cleaned with mild soap on a damp sponge. A dusting with baking powder can also work. I saw a fresh lemon rubbed over a smooth-grained leather to clean it in Mexico. It worked!

To clean suede, use a fine sandpaper or a stiff bristle brush. An art-gum eraser will also remove dirt. Grease can sometimes be removed with talc or pumice powder. Try a small sample first. Some commercial cleaners dry out the suede.

Deerhide, buckskin, and elk garments can be washed in a washing machine with mild soapsuds. While dripping wet, they should be allowed to dry on wooden hangers. Squeezing out water squeezes in wrinkles.

Leather can be pressed to remove wrinkles under a pressing cloth or heavy brown paper. Set a *dry* iron at the lowest temperature and keep it in motion continuously.

Do not use plastic bags over leather because leather needs air. Some bags tend to stick and discolor the leather. Also, avoid moth repellents. They stain leather.

The life of all leather articles can be extended with the proper care. Don't wait until the leather cracks or crumbles. Clean and lubricate leather periodically—perhaps twice a year.

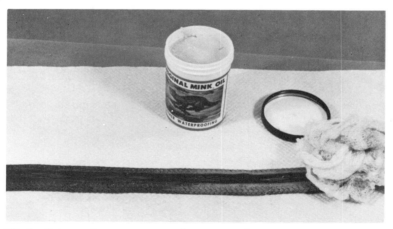

Mink oil is used to preserve and waterproof. It is utilized here to recondition dried-out leather. It should be applied liberally; allowed to stand for five minutes, and then excess wiped away. Wax then can be added.

6

THE STRUCTURE
AS DESIGN

Many decorative approaches to leatherwork
are structural, inasmuch as the leather surface that makes up the form itself is also the
decorative means. Weaving with leather is
one example, appliqué another. This differs
from decoration of leather surfaces with dyes
and carving as seen in chapter 5. A wealth of
decorative possibility opens up when leather
is used with leather.

PLAITING

Plaiting, or braiding, is the use of interwoven strips of leather to make linear objects
such as belts, straps, and sculptures. Types of
plaiting were known to the American Indian

before the Spanish arrived with their elaborate techniques. Designs can be enormously
varied, so many that they could fill a book.
Only a few styles are shown, which are applicable for belts and wristwatch straps.

ENDLESS BRAIDING

Endless braiding looks like a mystery because
the ends are obviously not cut. The secret is in
passing the lower end through the slits to un-
wind the plaiting.

To begin, split a strap, or belt, blank into three
even sections with two slits, leaving a half inch
or more at top and bottom uncut. Notch the
top and bottom of each cut with a hole punch.
This eliminates bulk and allows for twisting.

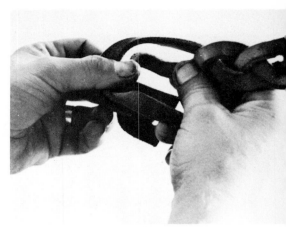

Then untwist the bottom by pushing the bottom through one of the slits, while holding on to the braid you have achieved until now.

Braid the top, as usual, as far as you can go without creating a jumble at the other end.

With the braid untwisted, continue to plait.

Again untwist the bottom, this time try the other space. Continue this operation until the piece is braided. The bights should all be the same size.

A belt illustrating this process by Ted St. Germain.

Another Ted St. Germain belt plaited with five sections.

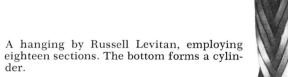

A hanging by Russell Levitan, employing eighteen sections. The bottom forms a cylinder.

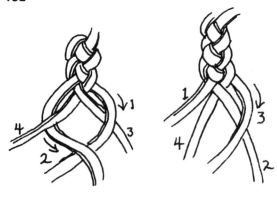

This diagram for a four-plaited "rope" is very common for making neckpieces. Each strand is indicated with a number.

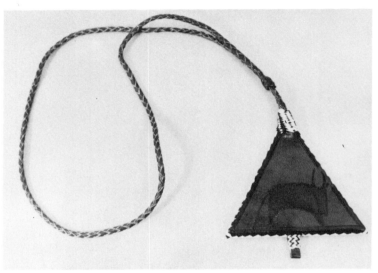

A four-plaited round strand attached to a pendant that was made in Ghana.

WEAVING

Since leather is a very tough material, it can be used where there are wear factors, such as for pillows or throw rugs. Sometimes, warp is of another material, or some kind of yarn, and the weft is leather. When leather warping is used as in Murry Kusmin's hang-ing, it is nonstretchable belting, or if it is the same kind of leather as the weft, the woven piece is inserted into a stabilizing body or frame so that edges can be tacked. It is also possible to knit, crochet, and use macramé techniques with leather lacing. Combining these with solid planes of leather is very effective.

A simple weaving technique that includes many variations starts with a basic unit with holes, this one a figure 8, and then permits the inter-weaving of strips of leather to unite the separate units. Strips are woven in and out of the pieces.

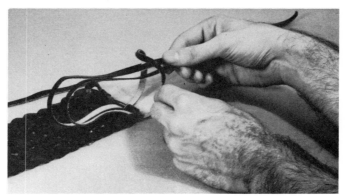

The end of the strip is cut and glued.

Strips of leather are attached for tying—or a buckle could be used.

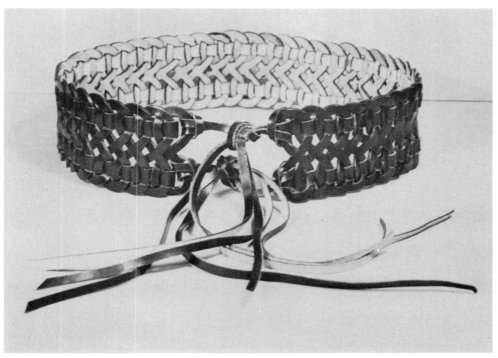

The completed belt. The figure 8s were die cut.

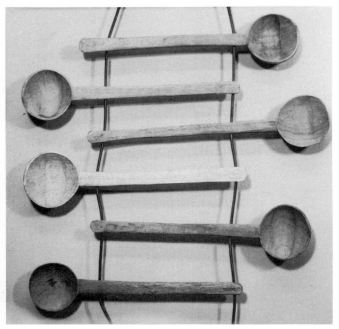

This woven hanging by Murry Kusmin starts with a warp of wooden spoons nailed to belting.

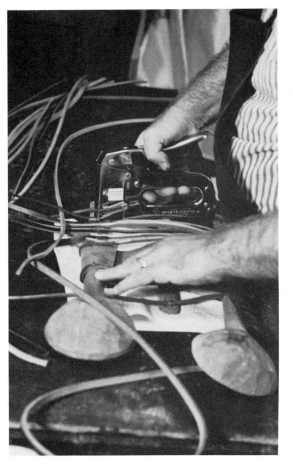

Murry Kusmin tacks belting strips with clinching nails to a piece of suede that will become a major part of the weft.

He staples the end of a weft piece to the top of the warp spoon.

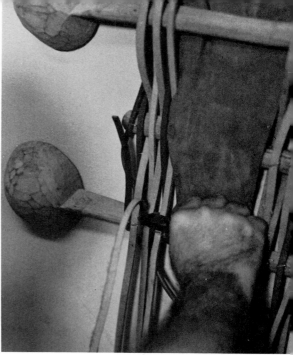

Then he interweaves that piece and other narrow leather strips of various colors of brown, in and out, around the warp (which are the spoons).

Murry clips off excess from the back after he staples each piece in place on the back of the spoon.

After the addition of two more attachments, plaited pieces, the hanging by Murry Kusmin is ready for its place on a wall.

"Tapestry Bag" by Murry Kusmin. Irregular strips of different colors (browns) of leather are interwoven and then nailed to a "frame" of leather to form a decorative panel for this elegant shopping bag.

Each strap of this bench is attached on three sides to the underpart of the walnut frame before weaving begins. The free end is woven in and out of the attached warp. Either the warp or the weft needs to contain an odd number of pieces, the other an even number.

Woven weed pot by Ted St. Germain. Leather strips are woven as if they were made of straw.

"Fallen Bird" tapestry by Murry Kusmin.

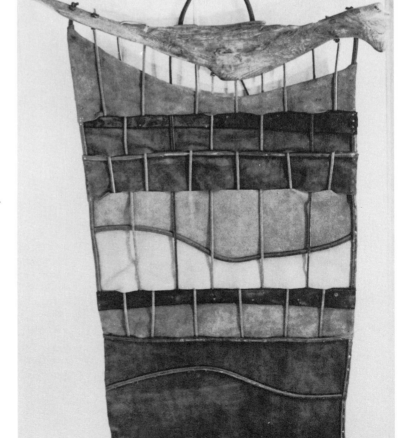

Model for ark doors made of belting leather of varying widths by Murry Kusmin.

APPLIQUÉ

Leather appliqué is the attaching of one piece of leather, usually of another color or texture, to another. The leather can be superimposed over the top or in reverse appliqué where the top surface is cut away in a design to reveal color and texture underneath. The colorful leathers used in appliqué are usually lightweight, else thickness can build up into a cumbersome piece.

Most often pieces are glued in place and then sewn with a sewing machine, or by hand, or else laced with leather lacing. When laced, holes are punched to accommodate the lacing.

In reverse appliqué the supporting piece is cut out into a weblike matrix, or pattern. Smaller, contrasting colored pieces of leather are glued into place behind on the flesh side to cover the holes, and then each part is sewn.

Symmetrical pieces are machine stitched in an appliquéd design by Jim and Karen Eagan.

Another version of an appliqué design functioning also as part of a pocketbook closing. By Jim and Karen Eagan.

Hand-carved pieces are hand stitched, glued, and nailed to a belt base. By Doug Shaffernoth.

Hand-stitched appliqué and reverse appliqué. When an underneath piece shows through a cut superimposed area, it is called "reverse appliqué." The two techniques are skillfully combined on a purse flap by Ben Liberty. *Courtesy Ben Liberty. Photo by Jeffery Boxer*

John Fargotstein's "Portfolio" is 36 by 24 by 5 inches deep. Pieces are appliquéd over other pieces. Note the precision of the hand stitching, and how the stitching and every color texture and shape integrates into a whole design. Although functional, this piece certainly is an art form. *Courtesy John Fargotstein*

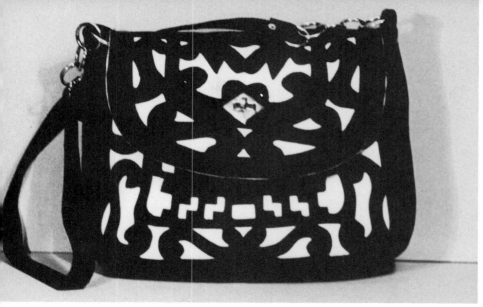

Almost in silhouette, a grid of dark brown suede is machine stitched over white, smooth grained leather.

Appliqué via cementing. Suede on suede. By June and John Anderson.

Reverse appliqué, machine stitched, by Ben Liberty. Note that edges of the purse flap and strap are hand stitched. *Courtesy Ben Liberty. Photo by Jeffery Boxer*

A container of copper, leather, and wood with a bone lid handle, 18 by 14 inches. John Fargotstein's appliqué is super-imposed and repeated around the body and on the top lid.

Machine-stitched appliqué purse by Ben Liberty. *Courtesy Ben Liberty. Photo by Jeffery Boxer*

A reverse appliqué "painting" in suede called "The Simple Orange Sun," by Murry Kusmin.

Appliqué pocketbook by Ben Liberty, using different texture and color accent with brass findings. *Courtesy Ben Liberty. Photo by Jeffery Boxer*

A hassock using both appliqué and reverse appliqué, by Ben Liberty. Top and bottom rims are of leather welting. *Courtesy Ben Liberty. Photo by Jeffery Boxer*

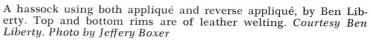

PATCHWORK

Patchwork is a great way to use small pieces and odd bits of leather. Pieces of leather are juxtaposed edge to edge to make a whole.

Usually, a pattern of paper is cut so that pieces will fit, as in a jigsaw puzzle. Then the leather is cut corresponding to each small piece of paper. If the parts are to be laced, then holes are punched around each piece, matching the correct number of holes for pieces that are contiguous. These parts are then laced. If parts are to be sewn, then edges are sometimes glued with rubber cement before sewing. If a piece is very large, parts can be glued to a skiver (thin lining piece) before sewing edges. The skiver should be the size of the completed form.

Hand stitches can vary from the running stitch, combination stitch, or cross-stitch. When using cross-stitches, make certain that crosses go all in one direction. And when lacing, keep splices of lacing on the underside. In both appliqué and patchwork, make certain that end threads are knotted and glued so that they do not loosen and pull away. Restitched leather rarely looks like the original.

Patchwork in a kit concept by Caldwell Lace Leather Co. that permits many interpretations on a theme. Prepunched split leather squares are joined by lacing in a buttonhole stitch.

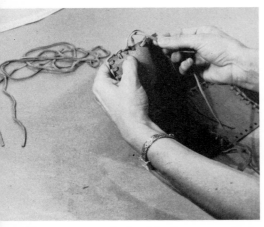

Edges are attached with the same single buttonhole stitch.

A button and beaded thong is used as a closing with the same wood beads as a handle.

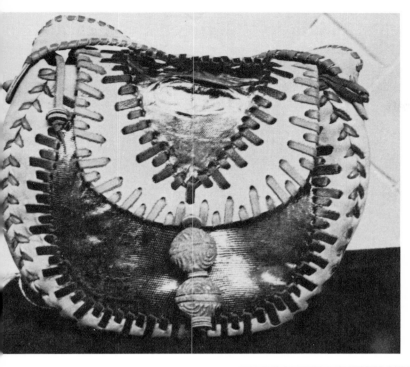

A unique purse in lizard and leather patchwork, attached with lacing. By the Girasol group.

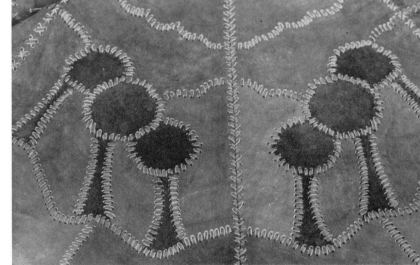

Detail of a cape showing the skin and grain side contrapuntally varying the texture. Parts are attached with lacing.

Detailing on the reverse side. Note that wherever there is stitching, a reinforcing strip is glued over the point where separate pieces are juxtaposed.

A magnificent patchwork cape by the Girasol group.

Two patchwork pillows by Ed Ghossn and Florence Sohn for L'Insolite, Inc.

A Girasol patchwork pillow, machine stitched, but with a reinforcing web in the approach used by the Girasol group.

Leather welting is used to join patchwork sections of this Mexican pillow.

Patchwork of random scraps is overlapped and machine stitched. Note the cloutage treatment on some of the pieces. Pillows by Smithskin Clothes.

CLOSINGS

Some concepts for closing a pocketbook, briefcase, book, and door are given here. Other examples appear throughout this text. Buckles can be made of leather, metal, bone, elastic, or wood, and are attached to the base usually with a leather strap and rivets, snaps, or by handstitching. Other closings are designed into the piece using the leather design itself as a means for closing the form. There is no end to inventiveness here. Some unique approaches start with a piece of paper and scissors.

Here, too, a double handle becomes the closing in this quilted purse by Ben Liberty. *Courtesy Ben Liberty. Photo by Jeffery Boxer*

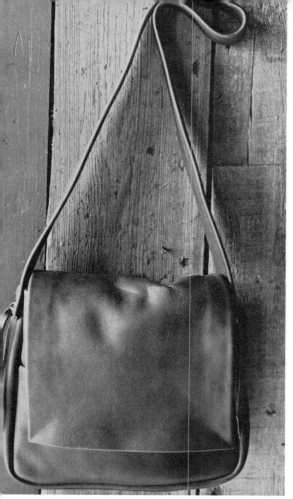

The weight of the flap closes a simple, functional bag, by Ted St. Germain.

Here, too, the flap of the bag needs no clasp. By Yael-Lurie and Jean Pierre Larochette.

A brass thingamajig acts as a tension clasp for this briefcase, by Jeff Slaboden.

Uniquely, the shoulder strap helps to function as a slot for the purse lid. By John Anderson.

The length of this mirror can be adjusted by moving the buckle a notch. Mirror by Richard Rosengarten.

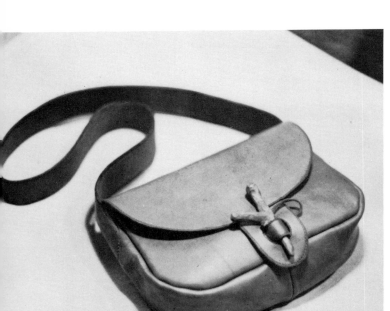

A scrap of tree branch locks the latch on this purse, by Jim and Karen Eagan.

Another work of art by John Fargotstein utilizes two sculptured "handles" for this purse. *Courtesy John Fargotstein*

Jeff Slaboden's book is belted and buckled, a symbol of privacy.

A piece of "sole" leather is carved and decorated by burning, by Yael-Lurie Larochette. It forms the latch along with a piece of lacing and a bead. The black background is colored with asphalt diluted with benzine.

To change the picture, merely unbuckle the strap. By Richard Rosengarten.

Locked up for safekeeping. A holder by Ted St. Germain.

Another interpretation of locking the bottle away from temptation, by Ted St. Germain.

A director's chair attached on the back with a cross-stitch. By Jeff Slaboden.

A frontal view.

The handle becomes the closing of a tubelike purse that adjusts in size to its contents.

Both latch and hinge are of leather with screws used as attachments, with hinge sporting a brass pin. Both are on the same door and are the creation of Murry Kusmin.

MURRY KUSMIN LAMINATING A POT ➡

Murry Kusmin stamps some two-inch-diameter circles and a second smaller circle to form donuts out of twelve-ounce vegetable-tanned cowhide. Note that pieces are not cut close together because shapes in between become other objects, such as sculptures, bracelets, and barrettes.

7

Laminating

and Forming

Although leather comes in limited thicknesses, it can be built up to almost any height (depending on wall thickness) by laminating layers. Beautiful sculptural effects can be carved into the leather as into a solid block. Only vegetable-tanned leather can be used because it can absorb water. By soaking it, leather then can be stretched, molded, and shaped over a form. When dry it assumes its new contours, unless wet again and re-formed.

LAMINATING

All kinds of contours can be cut, sawed, or stamped with dies from eight to fourteen-ounce-vegetable-tanned leather. To laminate one piece to another permanently, the surfaces to be adhered should be roughened and a contact cement such as Barge should be used on both sides. Pieces can be stacked over pieces until the desired height is achieved. Then surfaces can be modified by carving the leather with wood-carving tools or with various bits attached to a flexible shaft drill (for easy manipulation) or to a regular drill motor. Finishing completes the piece with coloring, if desired, followed by waxing and buffing. Boxes are a favorite; sculptures are another possibility.

175

Six donut pieces will be used to build up the box. Inner pieces are utilized to make other objects and one circle will become the socket part of the lid.

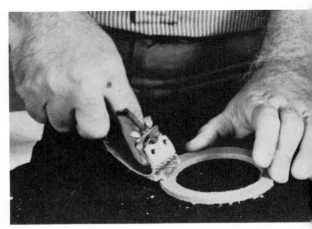

Surfaces to be laminated are roughened so that cement will grip better and form a strong bond.

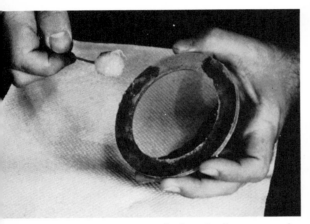

Barge cement is applied to both areas to be glued, and allowed to dry for at least twenty minutes before . . .

. . . attaching. The process is repeated until the desired buildup is achieved.

The pieces that just were attached are pounded before the next ones are added.

The lid consists of three circles. Now the "fun" part begins when the first sculptured mark is made into the lid with an abrasive bit (on a flexible shaft drill).

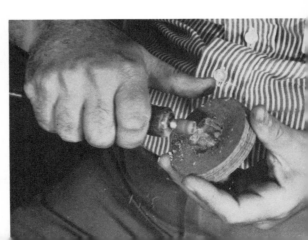

More carving is done with wood sculpture tools.

And further refinements are clarified with a sanding drum (on the flexible shaft).

Then Murry buffs and polishes with a muslin wheel by wetting the area first with a bit of water applied via a dauber, and then he applies beeswax for a polish and preservative.

The lid is scratched within the diameter of the socket. The socket is scraped and Barge cement is added to both lid and socket.

The socket is attached and pounded with a hammer.

Further polishing is performed with a larger muslin wheel using the same water-beeswax treatment as before.

A brass nail is hammered into the lid to key it to the base.

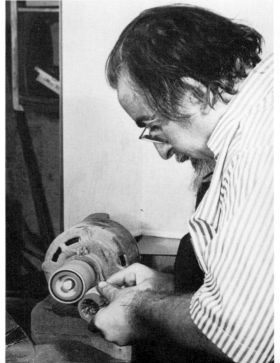

With the lid attached, Murry Kusmin sands the exterior sides on a rotary sander.

After more polishing, the pot is completed.

Laminated leather pots by Murry Kusmin.

Tops of three Murry Kusmin "refugee" pots, as he calls them (because he has a brass nail hiding somewhere in the sculptured cave of the lid).

Pot by Doug Muller. A different treatment is used on the lid by inserting strips into the top circle before laminating the second lid piece.

Note that Murry's tall pot is left in an irregular pattern. There are sur-
prises inside expressed through various carved patterns.

All shapes are cut via knife into a free form in Ed Viola's box. All carving was tooled with a knife as well.

"These Chains, Mine and Yours" by Murry Kusmin are interwoven and laminated rings.

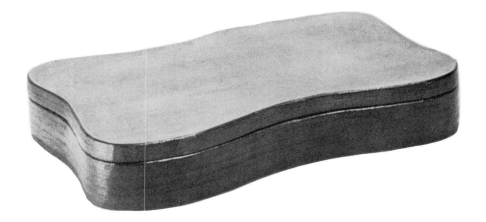

John Anderson's box, six layers high.

"The Devil in Me, Sees Me," a bas-relief by Murry Kusmin.

Box by Dick Muller, of eight-ounce cowhide with the top laminated of twelve-ounce cowhide. The flower is formed of four-ounce cowhide shoulder.

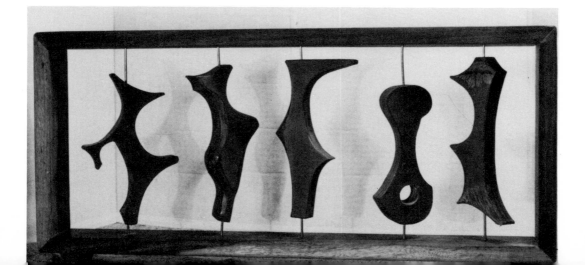

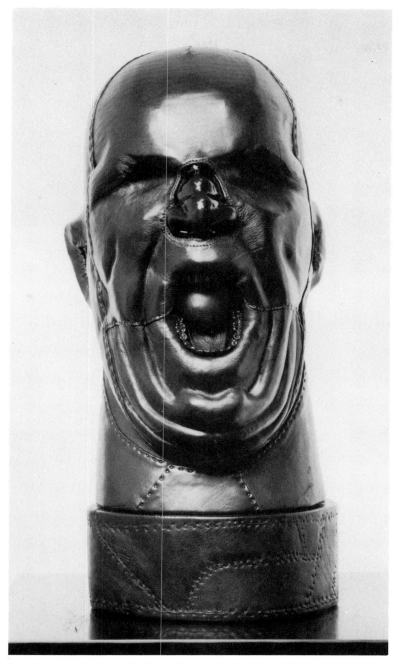

Leather is wet, stretched, and attached with nails to wood as in Nancy Grossman's head "M. L. Sweeney." 16¾ inches high. *Courtesy Cordier & Ekstrom, Inc.*

◄ "Dancers with Child" by Murry Kusmin. The figures can be pivoted.

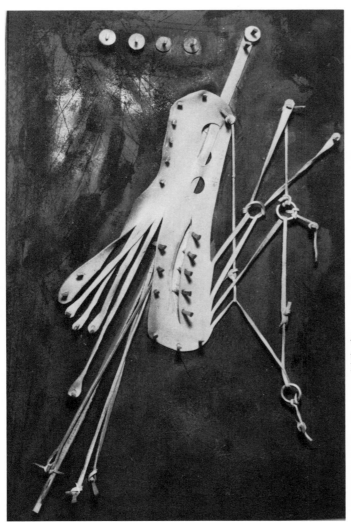

Wet leather stretched tautly to create a tension effect. This bas-relief by John Elfenbein is quite rigid.

FORMING

When leather is soaking wet it can be stretched, molded, and formed over a mold. Depending on the shape requirements, molds can be one- or two-piece. Only vegetable-tanned leathers can be formed because they absorb moisture. Leather should be soaked in water or, as Dan Holiday recommends, in a 50 percent mixture of naphtha to 50 percent mink oil. (If mink oil is not available, then use neat's-foot oil.)

Pine or any other soft, porous wood that can easily be carved and nailed makes the best blocks or molds. Antique hat blocks are great. Parts of blocks can be used and units coming off these old blocks may be combined into new shapes.

Nails are used to pull and hold the wet leather taut while it is drying; therefore, the should be rustproof—galvanized or alumi num.

Collar or saddle leather (shoulder o belly cuts) that is oak tanned, four to eigh ounces, performs best because it has greate elasticity. To test whether you have vegetable tanned leather, cut off a small piece and soa it in warm water for a few minutes. If it feel slippery and holds a fold, then it probably i a vegetable-tanned leather. Chrome-tanne leather will spring back and will not hold fold.

Stretching and forming has caught th imagination of artists who are making mar velous sculptural shapes. Weed pots, shape pocketbooks, sculptures, furniture parts masks, and bowls are some of the forms ex citing the imagination.

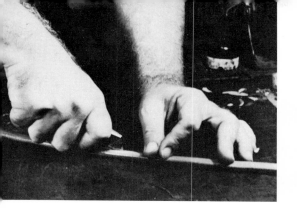

Industrial dyed leather belting is cut into "branching" structure using a razor knife.

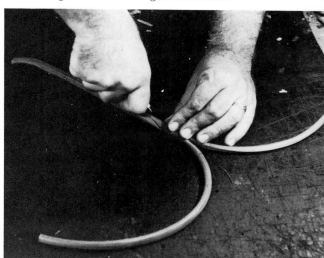

Branch sections are attached to suede-covered plywood with brad nails. An awl is used to start the nail hole.

Leaf shapes are individually cut from leather . . .

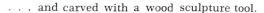

. . . and carved with a wood sculpture tool.

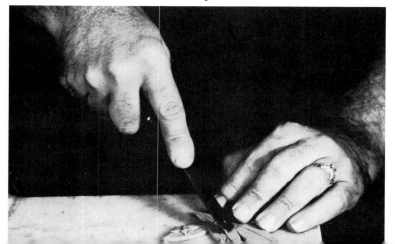

Then each leaf is soaked in alcohol for one minute, instead of water, because alcohol is absorbed sooner and permits better diffusion of color.

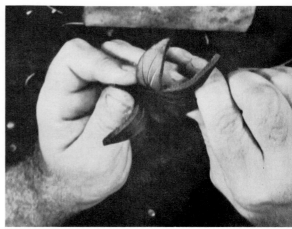

When sufficiently pliable, each leaf is shaped.

When dry, more color is added by dipping . . .

. . . and applied with a cotton swab. Powdered crystalline aniline alcohol-soluble color is used.

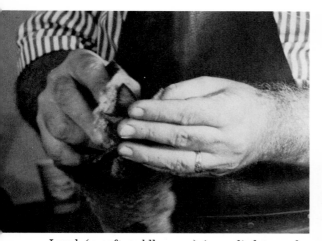

Lexol (a soft saddle soap) is applied to each leaf with a dauber.

Leaves are added to the branch structure with brads.

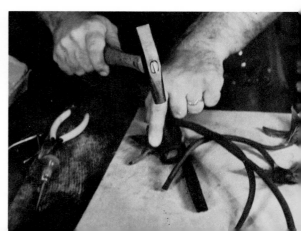

"Autumn Branch" by Murry Kusmin.

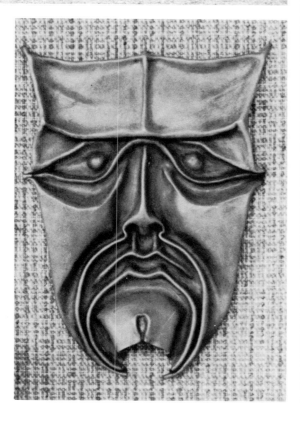

Two masks by Genevieve Barnett. Top grain, vegetable (oak)-tanned natural cowhide (three to five ounce) was moistened with a spray of water. Starting with the brow, the leather was shaped by squeezing and pushing. Creases were held until they kept that form. The leather was moistened as needed. After shaping, crumpled newspaper was used on the underside for support while the mask dried. *Courtesy Genevieve Barnett*

Mask by George Doran.

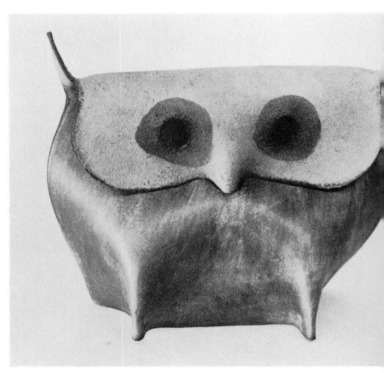

"Owl" by Richard Rosengarten.

"Mushrooms" by Genevieve Barnett. The top of the mushroom began with a circle. These were moistened, pulled, stretched, and pressed into the cap forms and then allowed to dry over a ball. Edges then were trimmed and skived. Stems were moistened, curled, and held in shape by wrapping them with string. Caps and stems were cemented and moss was added to complete the arrangement. *Courtesy Genevieve Barnett*

A bank made of formed leather. The back is locked and attached by the "flipper" hinge. The penguin mouth is always begging for coins.

FORMING BY MARY FISH

Photos Courtesy Mary Fish

Collar, shoulder, or saddle vegetable (oak)-tanned leather is soaked in water for four to five hours or overnight. It must be thoroughly soaked before molding.

Meanwhile, equipment is readied for molding: the form over which the leather is molded, a hammer, a canvas stretcher, and galvanized nails (so they won't rust).

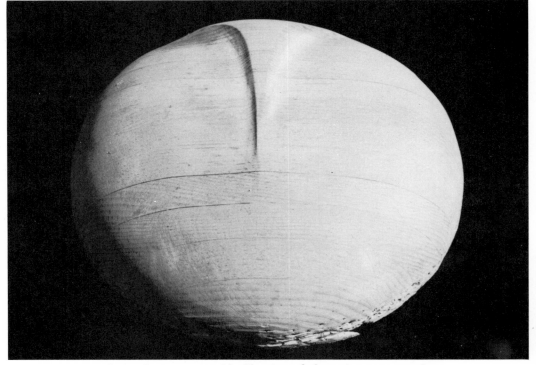

A simple one-part mold of laminated clear pine was carved.

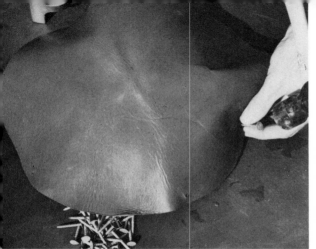

The wet leather is nailed to the mold on one side.

Then with a canvas stretcher, the leather is pulled on the opposite side until taut and nailed.

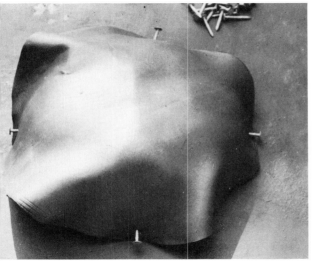

The process continues the same way on the other two sides. Nails are not driven all the way in, otherwise they would be too difficult to pull out.

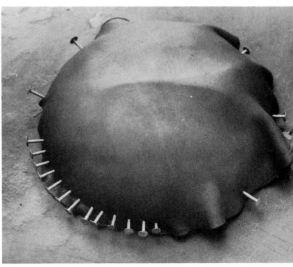

Working alternately one side, then another, proceeding around the form, nails are driven ½ to ¾ inch apart . . .

. . . until leather is nailed completely around the form.

At this stage the leather can be burnished with a spoon back, kneaded, pressed, and shaped to conform better to the mold.

When the leather has dried completely, nails are removed and the leather is peeled away from the mold. At this point it can be dyed, oiled, trimmed, and attached.

Mary Fish's handbag was combined with sheepskin, thonging, and part of a reindeer antler. *Photos Courtesy Mary Fish*

A two-part mold by Mary Fish is formed by laminating strips of clear pine. Roughing out is accomplished on a band saw, but finishing is done by hand with chiseling, rasping, and sanding.

A plug is used for the center in order to obtain a rounded lip on the leather.

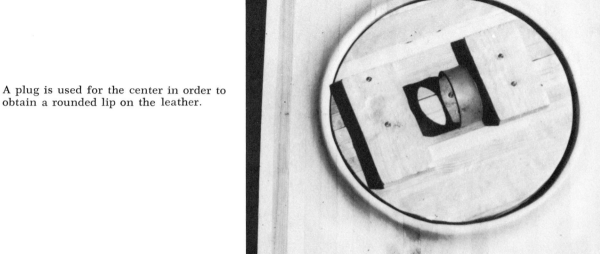

After the leather has been soaked, it is stretched over the form and nailed with galvanized nails to the mold base. The plug is forced into the center to push the leather down and form a lip. *Photos Courtesy Mary Fish*

FORMING A PAPERWEIGHT BY ED VIOLA

Lead BB shot and wet crumbly plaster of Paris are mixed together and centered in a square, rectangle, or circle of wet leather.

The wet piece is twisted and folded into a sack shape.

Again the form is moistened. Then it is tied with a rubber band and moistened once more while folds are rearranged and the whole piece is shaped and twisted.

When dry, excess is trimmed with a sharp knife or band saw.

When the bottom is trimmed flat and sits squarely, a small piece of ten to twelve-ounce cowhide is used as a base. The contour of the piece is traced.

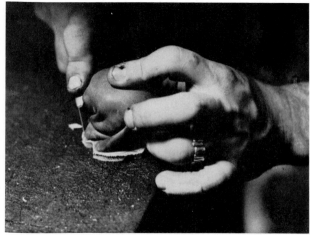

Excess is trimmed away. Cement is added to top and base and attached. Edges are trimmed again, sanded, and the entire piece is painted with dye. Edges are colored with ink.

After polishing, Ed Viola's sculptural paper-weight is ready to sit down on the job.

Formed weed pot by John Cederquist. *Courtesy John Cederquist*

Horsehide with hair is used for a box by Dick Muller.

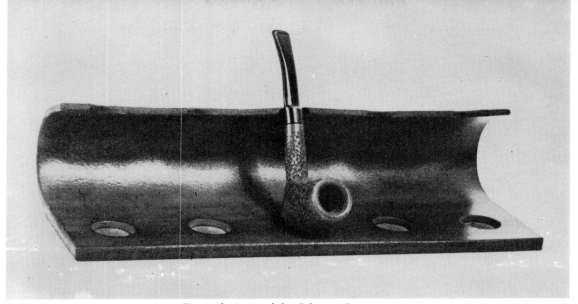

Formed pipe rack by John Anderson.

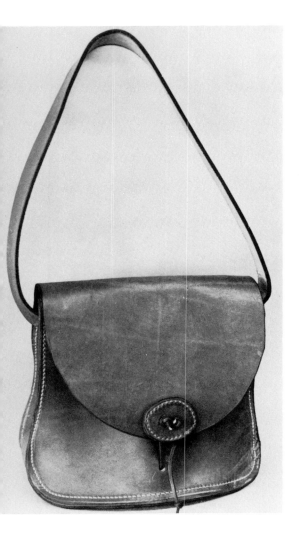

A hip-hugging bag that sits on the contours of the hip, by Ed Viola.

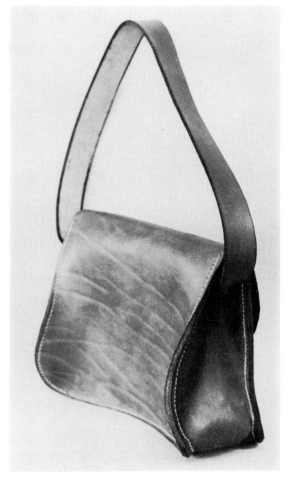

Jeff Slaboden's free-form cocktail table that utilizes a leather base (wet formed).

Murry Kusmin's "Quiet Bells" revolve around brass pins.

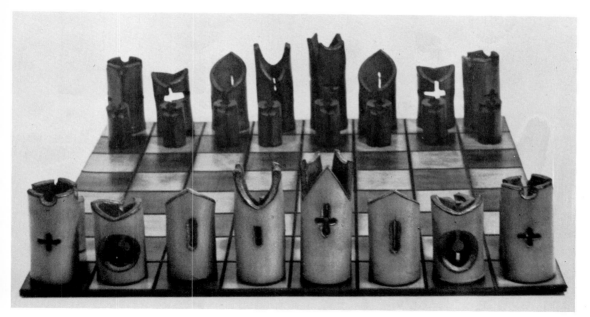

Chess set by John Anderson.

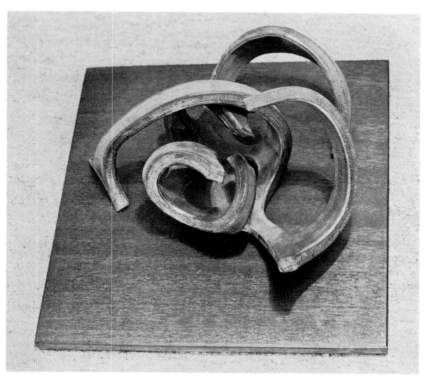

"Waterhole" by Murry Kusmin.

8

Adding Something Else to the Surface

Leather can be most decorative when a different color leather is embroidered or woven through it. Metal, beads, fur, feathers, wood, bone, plastic, and paper have also successfully been combined with leather. Some of these materials harken back to ancient tradition. Fur, bone, wood, feathers, and beads made of shells and stones have been used with leather before written history. Yet, contemporary artists have utilized these materials with remarkable innovation in the spheres of both fine and decorative art. Nothing is new about the techniques of how to use leather (and in combination with other materials), but the imaginative use of design places these pieces in the avant-garde of today's world.

EMBROIDERY

Embroidery with leather usually involves running narrow, thin strips of leather through the background piece in a weaving approach, or it is actually using embroidery stitches with exceedingly thin strips of leather as in the Moroccan and Malian pieces. Related to the latter is embroidery using henequen fibers as seen in the Mexican bag belts, or even using linen, silk, or cotton embroidery threads.

Where leathers are to be embroidered with thonging strips, slits need to be cut into the background piece and a lacing needle used to carry the thonging through the slits. When a heavy leather is to be embroidered, incised lines are made along the outline of the design. Stitches are then sewn inside the trough of the incision. A diamond-pointed needle eases the leather-piercing operation and works best for lighter leathers as well.

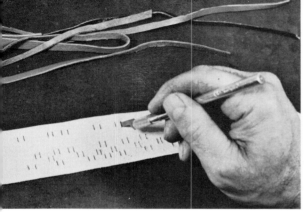

To embroider with leather strips, cut small slits in the base piece exactly the width of your strips.

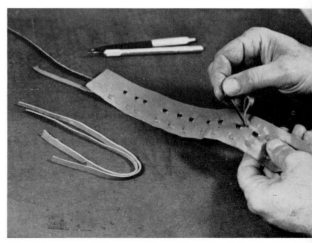

Thread your different colored/textured leather strips through the slits with a lacing needle.

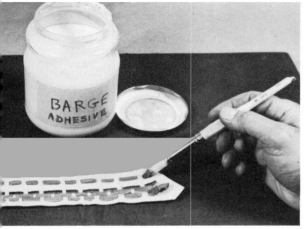

Cement ends.

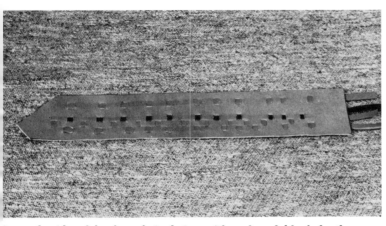

An embroidered bookmark in beige with red and black leather embroidery.

Leather lacing embroiders this Fulbe purse from North Cameroon, Africa.

A wallet from Morocco with an aluminum disk in the center.

Embroidering leather with leather is an ancient tradition found all over the east, west, and north of Africa. This is a contemporary Fulbe belt.

African bracelet. (Exact source unknown.)

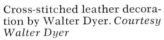

Cross-stitched leather decoration by Walter Dyer. *Courtesy Walter Dyer*

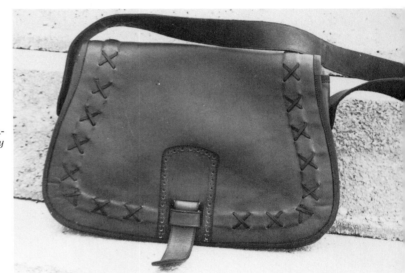

An elegant bench trimmed in leather and embroidered with silk on suede. By Florence Sohn and Ed Ghossn for L'Insolite.

Mexican split cowhide purse.

An old Yaqui Indian (Mexico) belt embroidered with cream-colored thonging and horn decorations hanging from the thonging.

A mirror embroidered in suede on suede by Florence Sohn and Ed Ghossn for L'Insolite.

A belt from Oaxaca, Mexico, embroidered with hand-twisted henequen yarn. The belt was incised as shown above before embroidering.

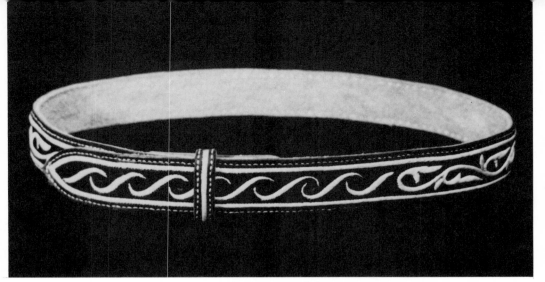

Another Oaxacan belt.

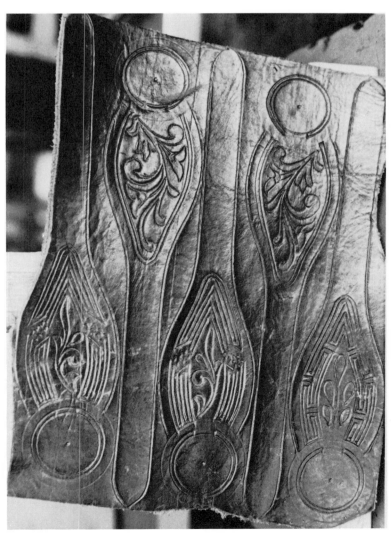

A tradition brought from Spain, this Mexican piece shows incising of
the design before embroidery begins.

Last of a dying art, this man's pocket-book from Oaxaca is inspired by Spanish tradition even in the use of cloutage decorations.

Some belt patterns from Oaxaca.

BEADWORK

Embroidery with beads can be done in various ways, as the following diagrams illustrate. The amount of beadwork will suggest the kind of application and the weight of leather. Beads can become rather heavy.

Diagram showing three of many different bead embroidery stitches.

a. Lazy stitch. Some beads are strung onto a thread that is attached to the leather at intervals. The needle dips into the leather, comes up again as beading is continued.

b. Reinforced lazy stitch—every other bead is threaded twice, before and after attachment to the leather.

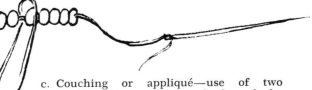

c. Couching or appliqué—use of two needles. One needle threads through the beads and another needle and thread attaches the strand to the leather at intervals.

Lazy-stitch beadwork in rosette form.

The completed necklace.

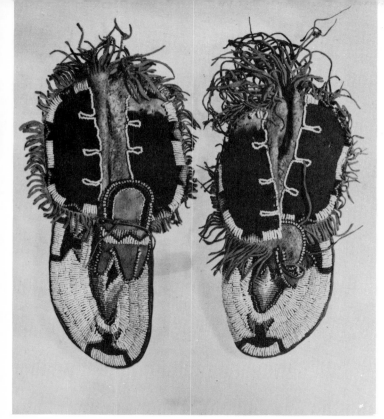

Lazy-stitch beadwork on a pair of Indian moccasins. *Courtesy The Museum of the American Indian, Heye Foundation*

Sioux moccasins using lazy-stitch and appliqué beadwork. The left one is 10½ inches long. *Courtesy The Museum of the American Indian, Heye Foundation*

East African apron, perhaps Masai. The leather is poorly tanned.

LAMELLÉ

A rare type of embroidery with thin pieces of metal strips is called *lamellé*. The metals usually were thongs made in gold, silver, brass, copper, and pewter. I have not seen examples recently, but remember admiring, many years ago, a very handsome Moroccan purse embroidered with pewter.

Slits would have to be made to allow the passage of the metal through the leather. Each stitch could be a separate piece of metal with ends bent back like a staple from a stapler.

Pounding the final result also would be necessary.

CLOUTAGE

Cloutage used to belong to the obsolete class of decoration much as lamellé, but there has been a revival. Cloutage is the use of fancy metal nails, rivets, eyelets, and grommets to decorate leather.

The proper tools need to be used as required by each adornment. These metal units should be organized into linear arrangements and/or shapes or clusters.

To attach a rivet for cloutage work, press a hole in the leather the size of the outer section of the rivet shaft.

Place the smaller part through the hole.

Add the cap.

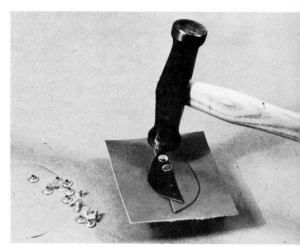

While the piece is sitting on a metal base, hammer the two parts together.

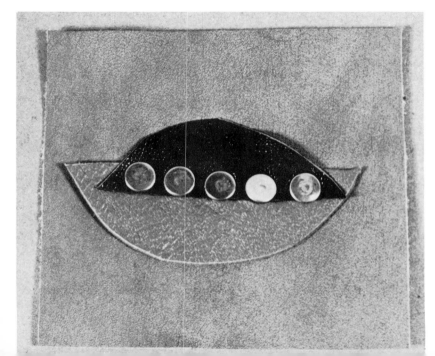

A cloutage ornament.

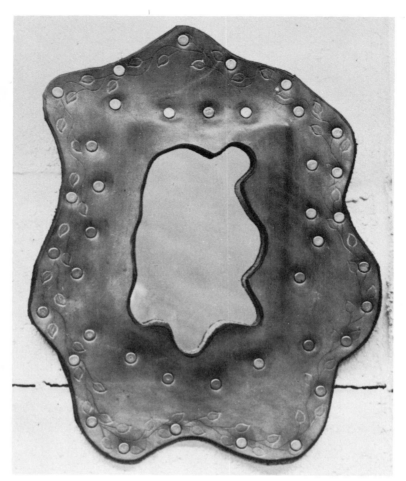

A mirror with stamped decoration and rivets used in a cloutage treatment. By John Giordano.

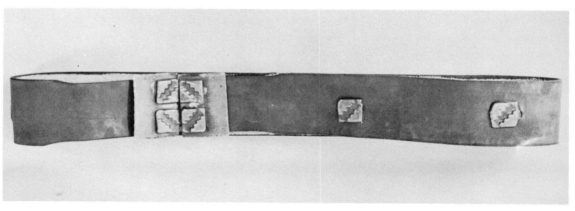

Repoussé copper ornaments combined with leather.

FRINGES

Fringes seem to belong to leather, perhaps because it softens an edge, solves a hemming problem, or because it does not ravel. There is no trick to creating a fringe. Usually all that is required is to cut parallel strips with a leather shears, paper cutter, or sharp knife.

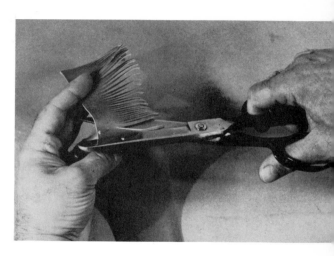

Cutting a fringe with leather shears.

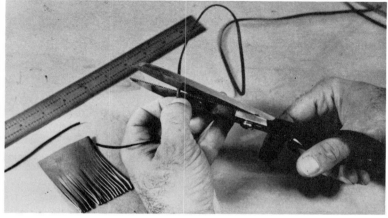

Lacing lengths that will act as loops for the fringe are cut.

Cement is applied to both sides at the top only.

The lacing loop is added.

The loop is rolled into the fringe.

Beads are strung on wire and the wire is wrapped around the fringe. Ends of the wire are tucked into the fringe seam.

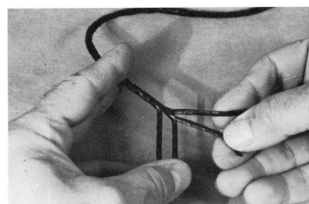

A four lace braid is plaited.

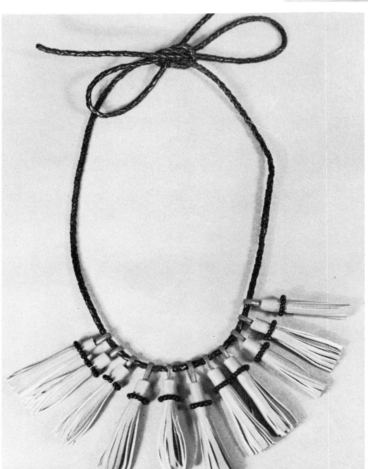

The complete fringe necklace.

Container by John Fargotstein. *Courtesy John Fargotstein*

An embroidered and fringed mirror by Florence Sohn and Ed Ghossn for L'Insolite. Background is dark brown suede; embroidery and fringe are cream-colored suede.

BUTTONS

Buttons and other shapes can be braided from thonging. Leather buttons are as old as buttons themselves. There are many approaches, all variations on the braiding theme. One is detailed here. Buttons also can be cut from heavy leather and holes pierced to accept sewing them onto garments, pillows, purses, etc.

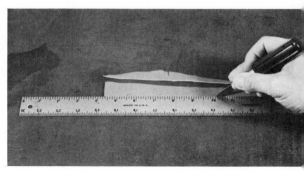

A button made with a scrap of leather rolled out of a long, narrow, triangular piece that is being cut here.

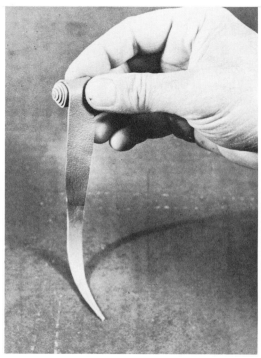

The piece is rolled, wide end first.

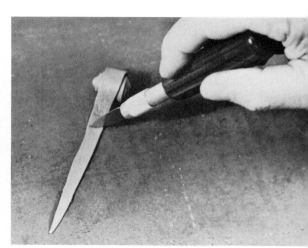

Two slits are cut about 1½ inches from the end.

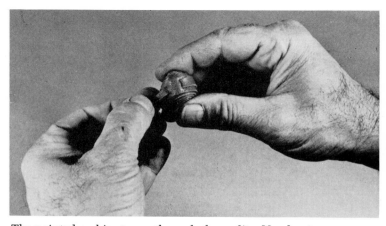

The pointed end is strung through these slits. No glue is necessary.

The completed button is attached by sewing it to the object between the two slits or by making a slit in the object, threading the pointed end through it, and sewing the point on the back of the object.

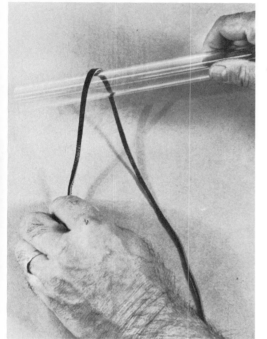

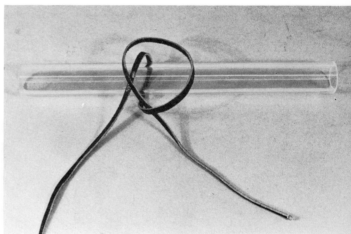

Plaiting a button in an "easy to see" way, around a rod.

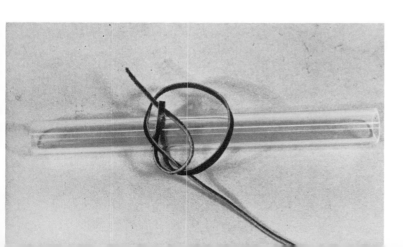

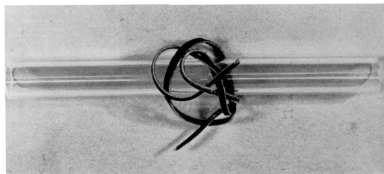

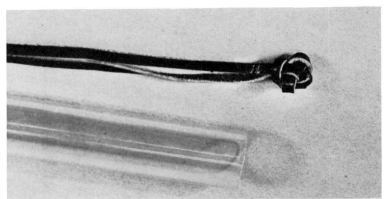

The completed button.

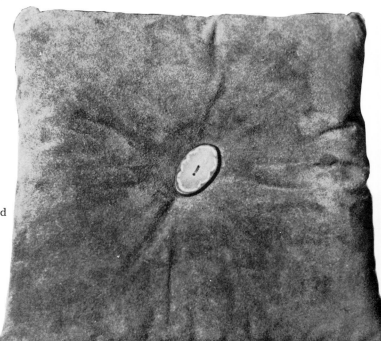

Pillow of split cowhide using a tooled leather button. By Jean Valenti.

BUCKLES

Buckles can be cut from heavy leather twelve to fourteen ounce or #12 or #14 iron, laminated with several thicknesses of leather; or metal belt bases can be covered with thonging in many different patterns.

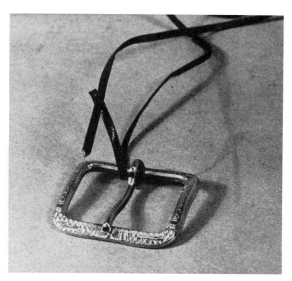

Buttonhole stitch lacing used to cover a buckle is begun by making a slit in the end of the lacing and stringing the lacing through the slit.

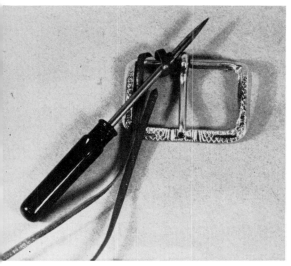

A fid points the way for the next step.

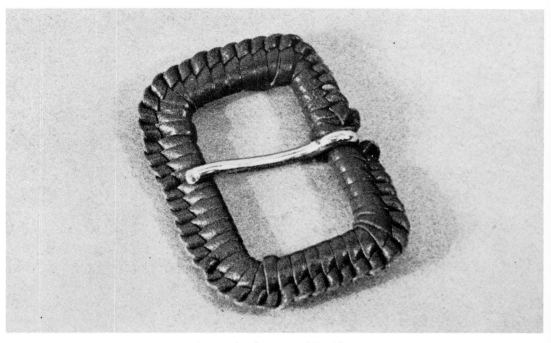

A completely covered buckle.

Some ready-made handcrafted buckles. The variety available today is enormous. Some sources are listed in the Supply Sources section of the book.

LEATHER AND OTHER MATERIALS

Feathers, fur, wood, bone, and shell have always been combined with leather. Fur and bone are relatives, perhaps emanating from the same animal. They seem to belong, but so do feathers, wood, shells, and stones. Beautiful forms also have been combined with wood. Some are wet-formed over a wood base, the same base incorporated into the finished piece. Other shapes, such as weed pots, are formed separately and then combined with a carved wooden piece. Attachment is by gluing, use of hardwood pegs, or with nonrusting nails.

Leather and plastic are a new approach with often startling contrast. Here again glues such as epoxies are probably the best adhesives. Acrylic sheeting can be heat-softened and formed directly into a hardened leather piece or formed in the same two-part mold as the leather. Before placing a hot, limp sheet of acrylic over the wooden form, drape the wood with two or three thicknesses of soft flannel, remove the wrinkles, heat the acrylic until it is limp, and immediately drape it over the flannel-covered mold. Apply pressure with a flannel-covered "cover" until the acrylic has cooled. Trim, polish edges, and combine it with the leather. (I haven't seen this process done with leather, but it is feasible.)

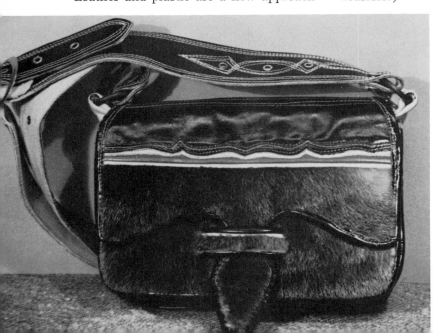

Fur and appliqué in patent and full-grain leather are combined in this man's purse from Medellín, Colombia.

Calfskin with hair on in a briefcase by Ben Liberty. *Courtesy Ben Liberty. Photo by Jeffery Boxer*

Container with leather, fur, and date pits by Joy Lobell. *Courtesy Joy Lobell*

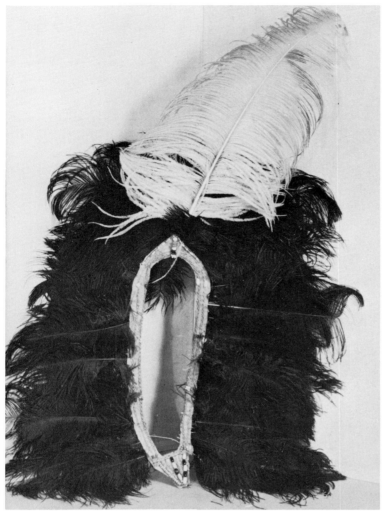

A Masai ceremonial headpiece of ostrich feather, leather, and bead, hand stitched with handmade palm thread.

Cabinet of wood and leather by John Cederquist. *Courtesy John Cederquist*

Mirror by John Cederquist. *Courtesy John Cederquist*

Weed pot of wood, leather, fibers, and feathers by Gregory Tamminga.

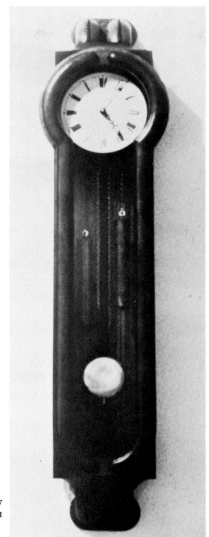

Clock of leather and wood by John Cederquist. *Courtesy John Cederquist*

Mary Fish's formed leather and plastic bas-relief. *Courtesy Mary Fish*

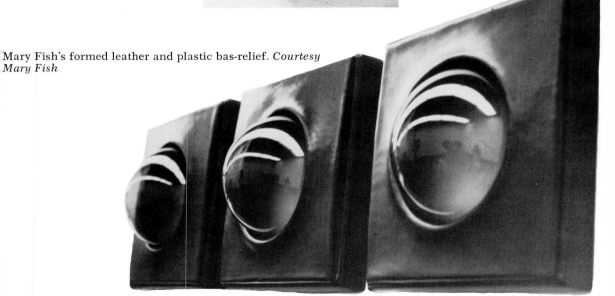

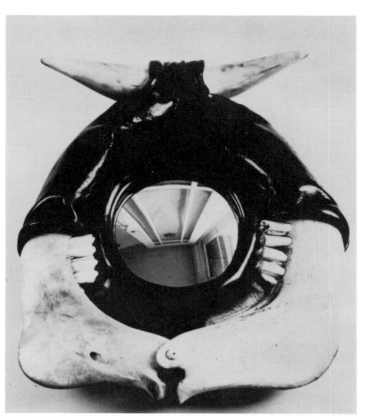

Hog-jaw mirror (12½ by 15 inches), by Nancy Flanagan. Made of formed leather, bone, horn, and a convex mirror. *Courtesy Nancy Flanagan*

Back detail of Nancy Flanagan's mirror. *Courtesy Nancy Flanagan*

"Black Flower" by Michael Sandle (6 by 4 feet) of leather, wood, Formica, and polyurethane paint. *Courtesy Michael Sandle*

A folk art piece dating back to 1820 picturing a Saxony gentleman in church dress. Fabric is combined with leather and a watercolor drawing.

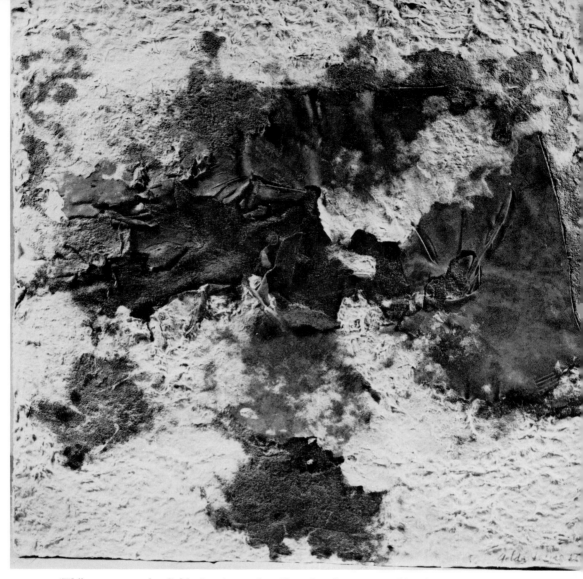

"Fl," a compage by Golda Lewis, made of handmade paper and leather scraps. *Courtesy Golda Lewis*

USE OF SCRAPS

There is no such thing as waste in leatherwork. Not even a half inch- by a half-inch piece is scrap. It can be made into a bead! The smallest pieces can become hair barrettes, watchbands, rings, bracelets, buttons, buckles, mosaic pieces for baskets, boxes, and bottles.

Slightly larger pieces can turn into sculptural elements and parts for a collage. Some sculptures and collages are included here in the scrap department, not to degrade the form but rather to stress the importance of saving every little piece of leather.

Any technique goes when expressing an idea through the medium of leather. Wet-forming, stretching, laminating, carving gluing, nailing, sewing—in fact all skills can be employed. Other materials can be combined with leather as well. Leather is no longer important as the structure of an object; it is a medium that is transformed to communicate something significant.

The smallest pieces of scrap leather can become a handsome necklace. By Ted St. Germain.

Every leather craftsman makes barrettes because it is a great product to cut from scrap. This selection is by Ted St. Germain.

A variety of bracelets by Murry Kusmin.

Key chains by Jeff Slaboden.

Leather mosaic scraps on bottles by Gerald Telmosse.

Leather mosaic scraps inset into a leather wastebasket by Foelich Leather.

Padded and small earrings in bright orange.

Scraps of dyed industrial belting make barrettes. Ends are nailed with clinching nails. By Murry Kusmin.

Sculpture or witty pendants are caricatures by Murry Kusmin.

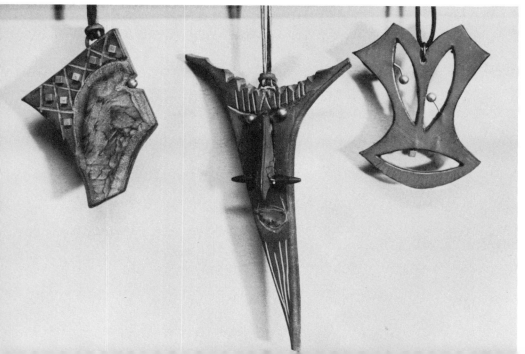

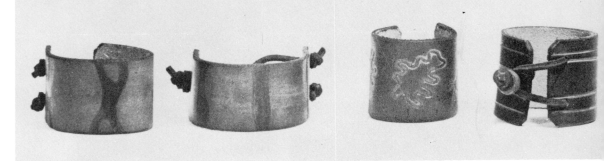

Bracelets by Jeff Slaboden.

Another decorative treatment using scraps, by Genevieve Barnett. *Courtesy Genevieve Barnett*

Scraps become collage through an ordering of parts by Genevieve Barnett. *Courtesy Genevieve Barnett*

A decorative plaque by Diane Shaffernoth.

"Tenement as Prison" by Murry Kusmin was made of what remained of a leather sheet (negative shapes) after dies cut into it. Parts are attached with clinching nails.

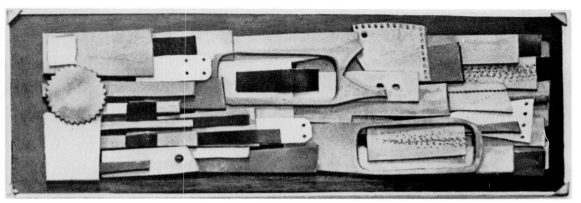

Collage by Genevieve Barnett. *Courtesy Genevieve Barnett*

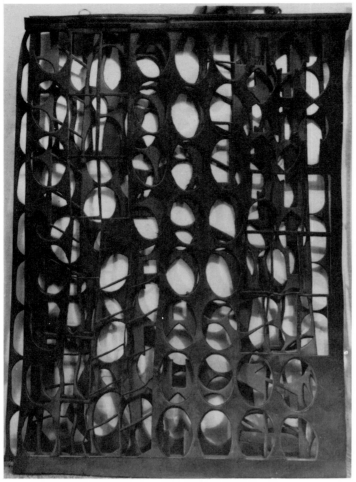

"Tenements with Fire Escapes and Dreams" by Murry Kusmin
is a combination of negative spaces.

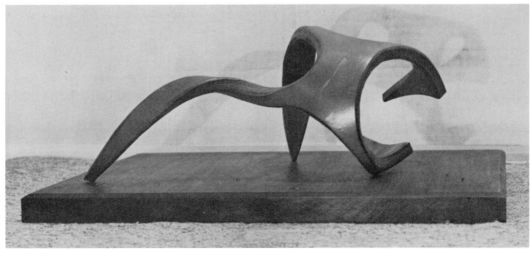

"Mother Is a Cradle" (and she is upside down), by Murry Kusmin.

Sculptures of scrap leather by John Elfenbein.

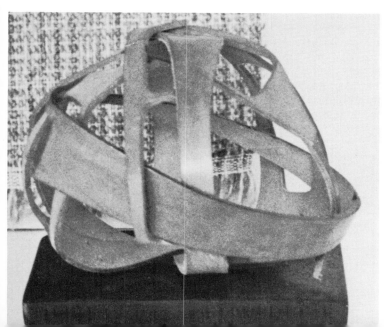

Sculpture of scraps by Genevieve Barnett. *Courtesy Genevieve Barnett*

9

Clothing

Leather is a great material for clothing and in many ways easier to construct than a fabric piece, if you consider that leather does not ravel and that leather garments should be of a simple line. Ready-made patterns, put out by major pattern companies, are available for leather sewing. Use your same size as for fabric. When selecting a pattern look for a design with a minimum amount of seams, gathers, darts, tucks, and frills. Choose one with a simple but well-constructed line that will dramatize the elegance of your leather.

Leather is usually less pliable than most fabrics, but it molds easily to the body and becomes a very comfortable clothing material because it breathes and permits the exchange of air and moisture.

TYPE OF LEATHER

Most leather for shirts, skirts, jerkins, dresses, pants, and lightweight vests runs from 2½ to 3 ounces. Outer garments such as jackets, coats, and vests could be constructed of slightly heavier leathers, up to five ounces. Most often leather sold for clothing is smooth grain, like cape and cabretta, or is suedes or splits of calf, goat, cow, sheep, deer, steer, pig, and horse skins. Whichever leather you select, it should be soft and pliable. Note in chapter 2 the section on estimating the amount of skin needed when matching pattern to leather. It is best to buy the pattern first, and if necessary try arranging your pattern on the leather to be certain you have enough. Pay special attention to the skin for imperfections, including extra-thin areas and very heavy sections. (Thin areas can be reinforced on the flesh side with iron-on mending tape.) Garment leather should be uniform in weight and color. If you need several skins, be certain that they match in every way.

If you purchase hides, or skins, by mail, order a bit more to be certain you have enough. If you have been dealing with a company for a long time, they may suggest an amount if you send kraft-paper duplicates of the main pieces of your pattern. For conversion from yardage to leather nomenclature, see chapter 2, "How Sole and Garment Leather Is Sold."

CUTTING THE LEATHER

Although leather structurally is omni-directional, experts say that it does make a difference which way a pattern is placed. It is similar to the warp of cloth, and like cloth leather will not drape properly if it is cut against the grain, so it is said.

In placing pattern pieces, then, the top part of the pattern pieces should be parallel with the skin's or the hide's shoulder or the bottom should be parallel with the bottom of the back, interchangably, but in that one direction. All cutting should be concerned with

the surface configurations, and pattern pieces should be set up as if you are arranging the pattern for matching plaids or stripes. Small trim pieces, pockets, and collars can be placed anywhere.

When a pattern calls for cutting two pieces, cut one at a time. Do not fold the leather and cut. Instead, if the pattern calls for a fold, cut another paper piece, a duplicate of that pattern piece, tape it onto the original pattern, cutting a whole, then, instead of a half, folded. Mark darts with tailor's chalk or a ball-point pen on the flesh side.

Patterns can be pinned to the leather if you place pins toward edges. Plasti-Tak is an excellent temporary adhesive. After kneading a small piece of the white plastic, place a bit on the pattern and press it in place on the leather. It will only adhere as long as you like and will pull away with no marking whenever you carefully lift away the pattern. (It is reusable.) Cellophane tape is often recommended, but it sometimes pulls away the leather's finish.

When cutting garment leather, the best tool is a leather shears, but a good sharp heavy-duty scissors will work also. Heavier leathers can also be cut with knives. Each time you cut a piece, label it as to which part it is. When cutting notches as for matching parts, cut V's outward rather than into the seam.

BASIC TECHNIQUES FOR MAKING A BERET

Design your pattern and arrange it on your leather. This is a tie-dyed suede skin. Then trace a line with a ball-point pen around each piece.

With shears cut around your outline.

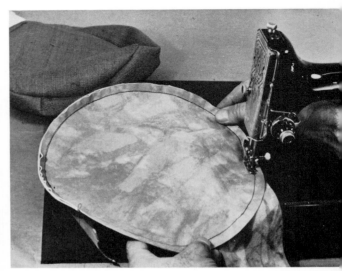

Clip or glue edges so each piece matches and sew as you would fabric. Fine stitches are used for fine textured, first quality leathers. A grooved needle is used.

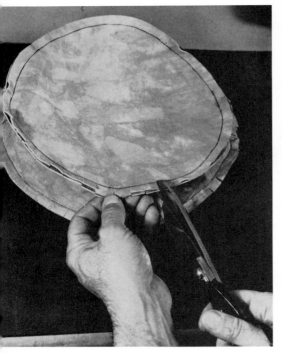

If a shape is curved, in order to keep it from pulling or bunching, slits or "Vs" should be cut up to the seam.

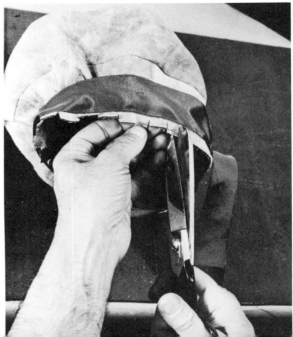

Cut and sew a lining the same way. Attach the lining by hand, or in this case stitch it along the edge. Grosgrain ribbon is used here as an inside hat band. Again, slits are made in the seam to ease tension.

A perky beret.

PIECING LEATHER

Study your pattern thoroughly. If your pattern calls for pieces that are very long, you may have to design new lines into the pattern in order to piece the leather together. You can conserve on leather by piecing, but take care to observe these precautions: Design your piecing lines to suit the overall lines and style of the garment. Never piece near a major construction seam such as a waistline, neckline, and point where the sleeve joins the shoulder. Match color, texture, and grain direction. Add an additional ⅝-inch seam to allow for the piecing line. Think about the type of piecing seam that will fit the design.

Piecing can be concealed when used for facings or undersections of sleeves and under collars. One obvious seam that is often used to define a design can be topstitched. Make a regular seam. Fold both parts of the seam to one side. Cement it down and pound it flat. Topstitch the three layers on the top side of the garment close to the seam line. Or, press the seam open, cement it, and pound down both sides. Then topstitch both sides close to the seam line. This will give you parallel stitching. Piecing can also be just a plain seam without topstitching; or for heavier leathers, just laying one piece over the other near the edges, gluing, and topstitching both.

SEWING

Hand sewing is performed the same way as for any leather article. Of course, machine stitching is faster. A regular sewing machine can be used for thin and medium leathers. Regulate your stitch size, preferably seven to ten to the inch. Adjust the presser foot for *less* pressure because even though leather is thicker than most cloth it is spongy. (Professional machines have a wheel instead of a presser foot.) Thread tension usually requires no additional adjustment, but if the thread loops on the underside or top, tighten the upper tension. Do not touch the lower tension. If the feed dog (little triangular projections that surround the bobbin thread and help to push the fabric along) leaves marks on your leather, use kraft paper underneath and sew it to the leather. You can tear it away later. It will prevent marking.

Cotton-wrapped polyester (Dacron) thread is best for sewing leather by machine. Some people use nylon, but it often builds up static and attracts lint. And cotton thread doesn't hold up.

Use sewing machine wedge-point needles sizes 11, 14, 16. Eleven for sheer suedes, kidskin, capeskin, and other soft leathers. Size 14 is for medium weight leather and size 16 is for heavier weights and extra thicknesses such as leather with linings.

Always use the same thread in both the bobbin and on top of the machine.

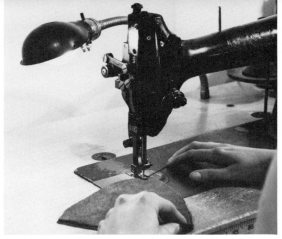

When starting or ending a seam, allow enough extra thread so that you can tie knots at beginning and terminal points to keep the seam from unraveling.

After threading the machine, sew as usual, allowing for ⅜-inch seams. If you come to an extra-thick area, ease the pressure by rolling the belt wheel with your hand. Don't force the needle to sew; you will break it. If a seam is too thick, cut or skive away excess on the inside. Once you sew a seam, that is it! Stitch marks remain, so be certain that the pattern fits and lengths are accurate. If you have doubts or worries, make a muslin garment first and adjust the muslin before cutting leather or sewing it. This is particularly true for making leather pants, where fit is critical. If you are going to line the garment, you may want to make the lining first, effect appropriate adjustments, and translate them to the pattern and leather.

If your leather stretches excessively, use rayon seam tape on the seam. Clip the tape to the length of your seam, tack it in place, and sew the tape and leather together. After each seam is sewn, pound it open with a mallet to make it lie flat and then lift it up again lightly and let it fall into place to relieve tension. Some seams lay better when glued. Use rubber cement because it remains flexible and won't become hard and brittle. If you need to reinforce an area for extra strength, use a contact cement such as Barge. Cementing should be done with restraint so that excess glue does not mess up the piece. If you should have some oozing of rubber cement, pick it up with a rubber cement ball, as you would use an eraser. Make a ball by spilling rubber cement on glass, letting it dry, and rolling it into a ball.

Both the right and wrong side of leather can be pressed with an iron using light-medium heat, but use a press cloth or several layers of kraft paper between iron and leather.

To reinforce seams, a fine quality of leather can be backstitched, but it is best to tie threads at the end of a seam.

Sewing curved seams requires the elimination of bulk or surplus leather. Cut triangular notches or slits into the seam with a sharp knife or leather shears around the curve, but do not cut all the way to the seam.

Darts as well as seams should be *opened* and pounded (and cemented) before sewing parts together.

Hems are never sewn, just turned back, pounded, and glued.

All other procedures are the same as for sewing fabric garments.

LININGS

Linings are not essential but may be more comfortable for clothing worn against the skin and for putting on outdoor garments. Linings are cut the same size as the leather pieces and the entire garment can be sewn except for facings. Linings become the facings for sleeves, but not always for necklines and openings. In this case appropriate adjustments in the lining are necessary.

Linings are cut the same size as the leather pieces. The entire lining can be sewn separately, except for facings and sometimes hems.

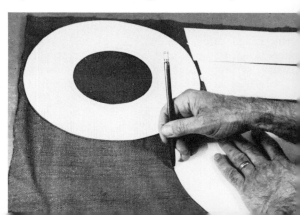

Stitching the lining to the leather can be done by hand around the neck (or neck facing), at the bottom hem of the sleeve, and, if it is a jacket, along the opening. Usually the bottom hem hangs free, overlapping and covering part of the glued bottom hem; but even this part of the lining can be stitched to the leather. Rubber cement can be used sparingly to assist in these operations.

A second method of attaching a lining that is used by furriers is to cut a bias binding from the same material as your lining, sew that to the leather, and then your lining to the bias tape.

OPENINGS

Zippers, snaps, laces and grommets, buttons and buttonholes, buckles and Velcro

This is a unique closing, "dart" and waistline adjustment, all in one, that is decorative as well. (The skirt is seen full length in chapter 5 on decorating with marking pens.) Each of four rows of lacing ends up as a bow closing. The lacing can be pulled tighter or looser. Next to the bow, the finger is pointing to cross-stitches that reinforce and decorate a slit dart on each side.

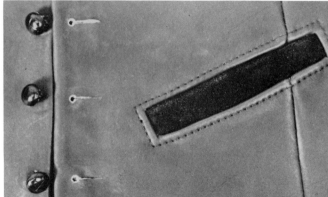

A buttonhole that is merely a punched hole and slit. The pocket is inset into the vest much like a pieced buttonhole.

The vest as it appears when buttoned.

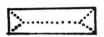 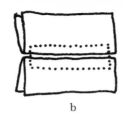 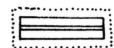

a
b
c

One way to make a pieced leather buttonhole.

a. Lightly draw lines as shown in the solid lines, outlining the outside size of the buttonhole. Cut along the dotted lines. Fold back each flap and pound them.

b. Place two pieces of leather that have been folded in half as shown on the flesh side of the garment. The dotted lines represent the buttonhole opening after flaps have been turned back.

c. Sew the half pieces around the area represented by the dotted lines. The stitching in this type of pieced buttonhole will show on the front. It is an easy approach. For thin leathers you can use the same techniques as suggested for fabrics.

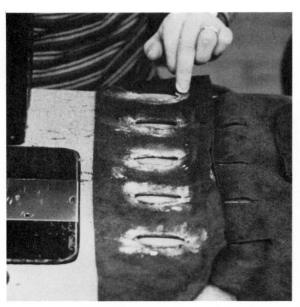

PIECED BUTTONHOLES WHERE THERE IS A FACING

This vest has a facing. To make pieced buttonholes, line up slits and glue edges back. Talc or chalk dust is used here to keep excess glue from sticking to those areas. Note that edges have been rolled back.

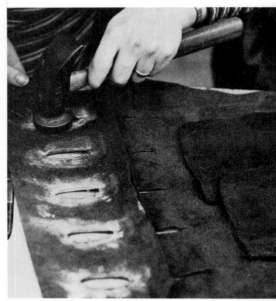

These edges have been glued and are now being pounded.

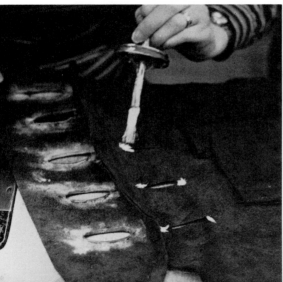

Contact cement is placed in the corners and allowed to set. A small triangle in each corner is folded back.

Two squares of leather are sewn, grain side facing grain side, on the top half and then on the bottom half of the buttonhole.

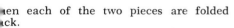

en each of the two pieces are folded ck.

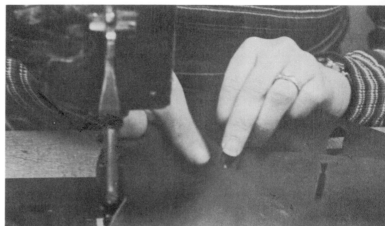

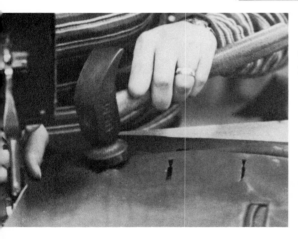

The pieces are glued on the back and pounded flat. The facing is tacked with glue.

The completed vest with leather buttons. At first the leather is stiff, but it softens up with use. By Walter Dyer. *Courtesy Walter Dyer*

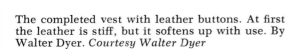

can be used. The procedures are the same as for sewing these parts to fabrics or for applying them to other leather constructions. More invention is possible with leather because you can allow raw edges to show without fear of raveling. If leather thicknesses build up too much, skive away areas to thin the leather. Do use rubber cement to hold parts in place for sewing. It is great for attaching zippers. Chalk dust or talc can be used around parts

you do *not* want to stick to the cement. It car be brushed away later.

Buttonholes can be just slits in the leather, particularly if it is heavy and no stretchy. Two other types are pictured and diagramed here. Buttonholes can also b trimmed with a buttonhole stitch usin; twisted silk or linen thread or cotton-covere polyester thread.

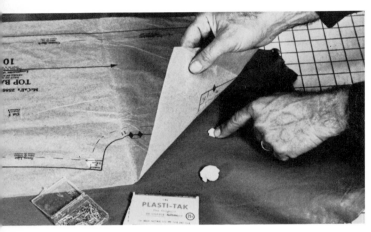

MAKING A JERKIN

Attach your pattern temporarily with a plasti putty.

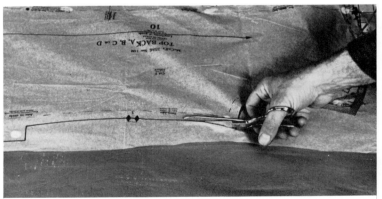

Cut the leather and pattern along the line or edge. Cut "Vs" out from rather than in from the seam.

Cut dart slits in the center of darts.

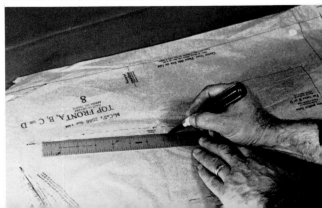

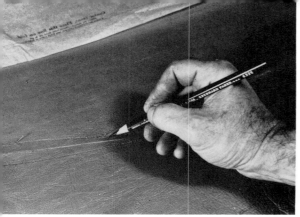

Indicate with pins and lines where darts should be.

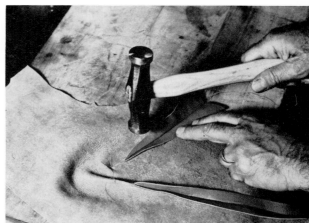

Follow sewing sequences as suggested in your pattern. Sew darts first. Tie all thread endings.

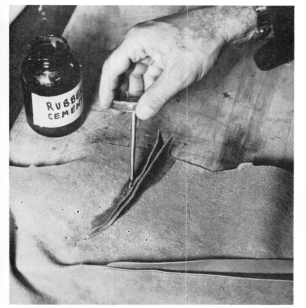

After each seam is sewed, glue them back with rubber cement.

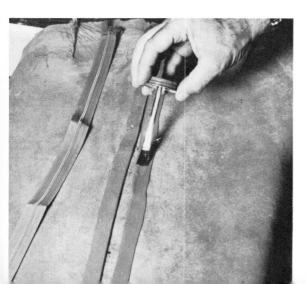

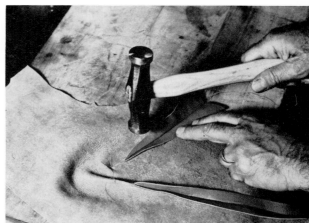

Pound the seam with a hammer.

Attach the zipper by folding back, and gluing the seam allowance. Then place rubber cement on top of the folded seam.

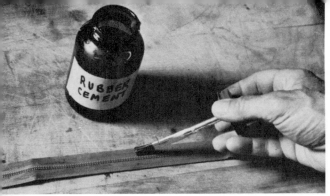

Place more rubber cement on the front of the zipper along both edges.

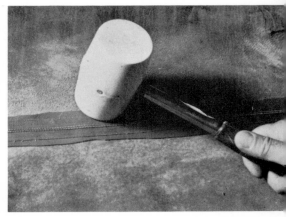

Place the zipper where it is to be and pound it. This acts as a basting technique, holding the zipper in place so that it does not slip while sewing. It also avoids making unnecessary needle or pin holes in the leather, which don't usually close up again as in some fabrics.

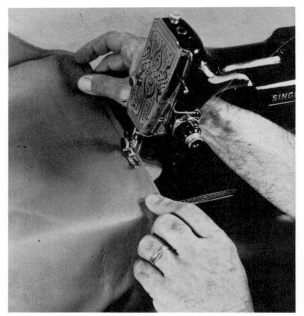

Sew the zipper in either an open or closed position. Since the zipper is glued when closed, you don't have to worry about it lining up in the end.

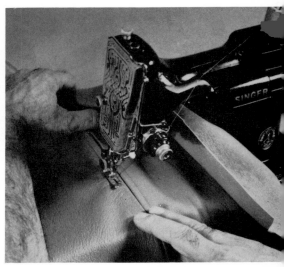

Attach facings and glue back.

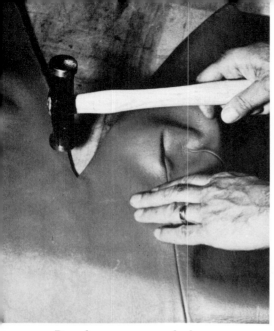

Prepare pockets by folding back edges, gluing, and pounding.

Pound seam areas and edges.

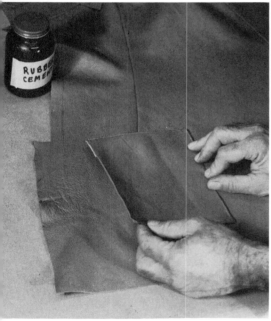

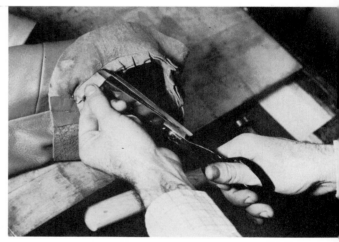

Slit or groove curved seams, particularly around the armpit.

Glue and attach in place (before or after lacings are added).

Make hems by merely gluing edges back. Glue becomes your needle and thread. The corners are being mitered here.

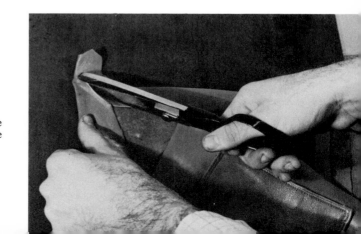

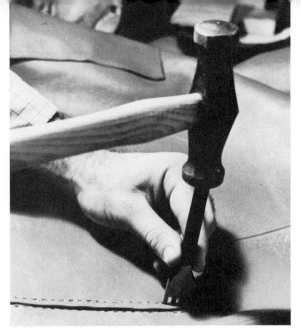

The pockets need a special touch. Thonging slits are pounded along the pocket seam.

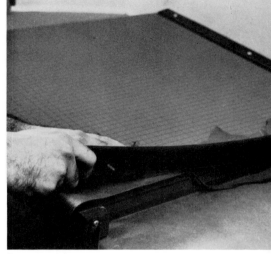

Lacing strips are cut on a paper cutter.

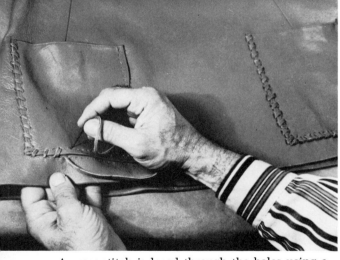

A cross-stitch is laced through the holes using a lacing needle.

The completed jerkin.

Bonnie Cashin has pioneered the use of leathers in clothing. Here is one of her latest high-fashion creations. *Courtesy Bonnie Cashin*

Patchwork jeans by Smithskin Clothes with rivet embellishment. Note the use of rolled leather as a button and the decorative overcast stitch along the waistband.

Every stitch is hand sewn on Doug Shaffernoth's jacket. Even the buttons are hand carved of bone.

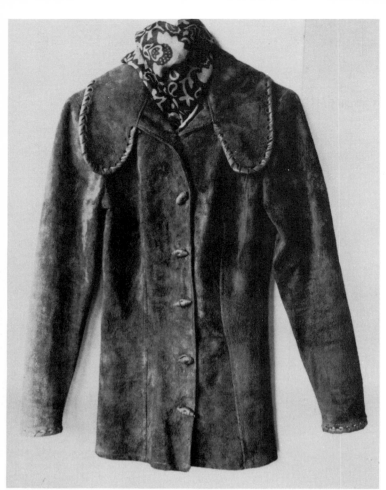

Overcast stitching is used to trim the collar and cuffs of this Smithskin suede jacket.

A cap and jacket utilizing metal snaps for closings by June Anderson.

June Anderson modeling her cape that is lined with a handwoven wool fabric.

Another of Bonnie Cashin's designs with leather—a complete costume from gauntlets to leg decorations. *Courtesy Bonnie Cashin*

A snakeskin skirt joined and edged with wool crochet and lined with silk. Grosgrain ribbon is used as a hidden waistband.

10

Footwear

Handmade footwear is handsome, long lasting, flexible, and comfortable. Styles can be distinctive and original, and since handmade footwear usually is constructed to fit the individual foot, comfort is assured.

Of all styles of footwear, the sandal is the most popular foot covering throughout the world, and has been throughout history, too. Everywhere civilization flourished, so did styles of footwear. At the height of classic Roman civilization, men's sandals were generally black, but women's were a variety of colors. Red sandals for men usually denoted that the wearer held a public office. Comedians wore a foot covering called a *soccus*, hence, the English word "sock."

Different styles of sandals indicated different ranks and positions in life. People could look at a stranger's feet and tell many things about him/her—status, village, job,

wealth. To this day Europeans still look down at a foreigner's shoes to seek clues to the passerby's identity.

CONSTRUCTION OF FOOTWEAR

PATTERN MAKING

Tools are simple—hammer, knife, oval leather punches, and a metal and/or wooden last are basics. The first step involves outlining the feet. Different symbols could indicate parts of the foot, for instance, the beginning and end of the arch, and various idiosyncrasies of foot structure. When outlining the foot, it is very important that the full weight of the foot is applied. As you outline, keep your pen vertical in order to get an accurate contour.

Making a pattern for sandals is simply

outlining the feet and then indicating where straps should start and end, then transferring the pattern to the leather, allowing one-quarter inch extra around the edge for working. Excess is trimmed later. Be certain to indicate left and right patterns, top and bottom. Making a moccasin or boot pattern is another story. Perhaps it is best at first to buy a pattern and make adjustments, or to take apart an old comfortable pair of moccasins or shoes to determine contours. If you wish to start from scratch, make your pattern from felt and put the pattern together as you would for leather to determine fit. Make commensurate adjustments. There is a great deal of trial and error in first attempts. (The circumference of the foot can impose problems in translation to a flat piece of oaktag or bristol board, which is your pattern.) Do not proceed to the cutting of your leather until you are certain of accurate measurements and that you are accommodating for seams.

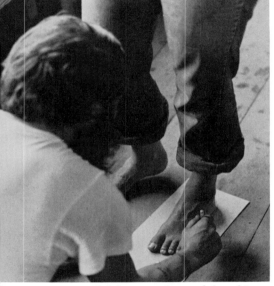

Patterns are a useful first step in sandal making. Ted St. Germain traces an outline around a customer's foot. Note that the person's full weight is on that foot and that his pen is held in an upright position. When a thong is used between the toes, place a finger between the toe to spread the area before tracing, as the toe would be spread around the thong. The arch begins at the ball of the foot and reaches its height midway, dropping at the beginning of the heel.

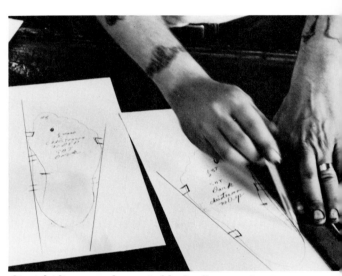

Straight lines are drawn to block off approximate size for cutting, allowing ¼ inch more all around. It is better to *cut more rather than less*. Note location marks of the straps and an indicator mark denoting the high point of the arch.

Refined contour of front and heel section is drawn.

The pattern is cut out.

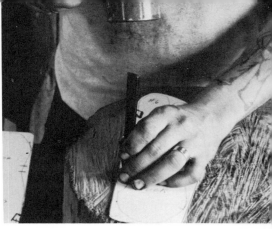

Thonging holes are cut with a bag punch one size larger than the strap width. (If the hole is too small, the strap will wear and break off there.) The punch size is usually ⅝ or ½ inch

SELECTION OF LEATHER

For most foot coverings that have a sole, you will need two kinds of leather. Bottom soles are usually hard oak leather 9 to 14 iron (No. 14 is one quarter of an inch thick), combined with either chrome- or vegetable-tanned top leather. Soles for sandals are in two parts—bottom and top. For the top soles use vegetable-tanned five- to nine-ounce cowhide. Cowhide can be wet-formed to conform to the arch, or it will conform by itself with wear. Straps for sandals should be from pre-stretched leather that is soft. Latigo or full-grain cowhide is very good. Straps should be cut about two to three inches longer than necessary and ⁵⁄₁₆ inch to an inch wide.

Slippers require lightweight leather of three to four ounces. Moccasins are a bit heavier—four to six ounces. Outdoor foot-wear such as boots should be from eight to fourteen ounces. Sheepskin is sometimes used for linings. (Sheepskin linings are cut from the same pattern and glued to the flesh side of the leather.) For conversion factors see chapter 2, "How Sole and Garment Leather Is Sold."

SANDAL MAKING BY DAN HOLIDAY

Dan Holiday does not make a paper pattern first. He finds that sometimes mistakes can be made in the translation from paper to leather. He has his clients place their feet directly on the leather and marks the (ten- to twelve-ounce oak) leather with a ball-point pen. Dye will eventually cover the ink marks. After cutting out the upper and bottom sole, Dan soaks (or coats) the soles with a softening mixture of 50 percent naphtha to 50 percent Mermac Mink Oil; if the mink oil is not available, he uses 50 percent neat's-foot oil instead. The mixture penetrates the leather without drying it out and hardening it as water would. Here he is flexing the sole to form an arch. All four pieces are shaped and allowed to dry.

ATTACHING STRAPS FOR SANDALS

Punch necessary strap holes into the top section of the sole. If an arch is to be formed, soak the leather (both sole sections) in water or in a 50 percent naphtha, 50 percent neat's-foot oil mixture until it is pliable. Shape them to conform to the arch configurations and let them dry.

Spread Barge cement on both parts of the sole. Let it stand for thirty minutes. String your straps through the appropriate premade holes. Adjust them by guessing the approximate length or depth needed, then press the two glued sole parts together. Use clinching (cobbler's) nails (⅜ to 1¼ inch) to cobble (anchor) straps, if used, to the bottom sole and then both sole pieces together. By nailing from the bottom to the top on a piece of metal, the curve end of the nail will bend back and hook into the leather. Even after the nailhead wears down, the nail will still be embedded in the leather, doing its job of reinforcement.

It is a good idea to cobble all around the sole ⅛ inch from the edge with ¾-inch extra iron clinching nails, each one inch apart.

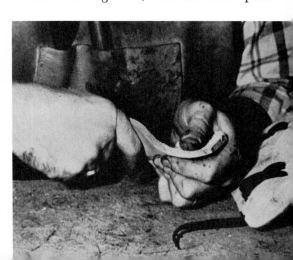

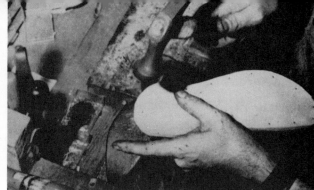

Sandal straps are cut with a draw gauge (a Strip Ease) or with a knife running along a steel ruler. Thonging slits are punched into the upper soles using a bag punch ⅝ or ½ inch, one size larger than the strap.

Sandal straps are strung through the holes of the upper sole after Barge Cement is put on the bottom part of the upper sole and upper part of the bottom sole. The soles are matched up and pounded with a hammer, then cobbled with ⅝ inch extra iron clinching nails for the sole and ⅝ inch extra iron clinching nails for the heel.

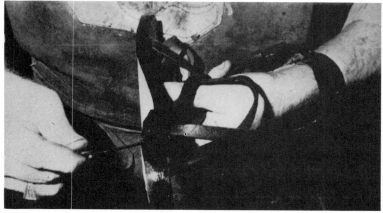

Edges are trimmed and sanded. Dan Holiday dips the whole sandal into a pot of dye because he makes so many. But for the occasional sandal, apply dye with a dauber. Dan uses Lincoln's dye (see Supply Sources). Next, edge enamel is painted on raw edges of the sole.

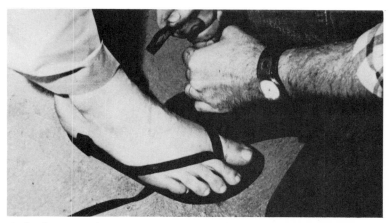

A final strap adjustment is made on the client's foot by pulling and loosening the strap. Rubbing mink oil with fingers on the strap in the area of the sole eases the operation.

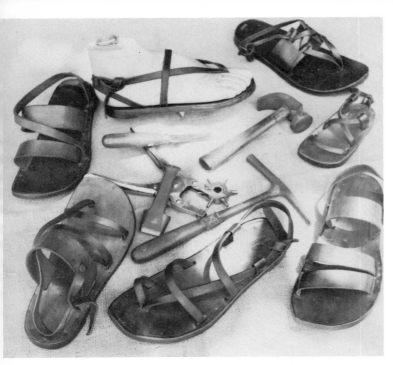

Assorted sandals by Dan Holiday, with tools of the craft. *Courtesy Dan Holiday*

A Dan Holiday sandal. Note that the straps thread through and between the top and bottom sole, and that they are adjustable by pulling or loosening the strap in sequence, much like tightening or loosening shoelaces. *Courtesy Dan Holiday*

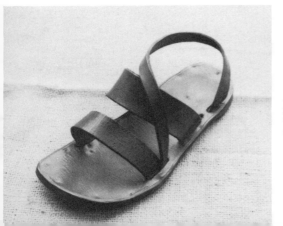

Another Dan Holiday sandal. In this model once the straps are adjusted, they are cobbled so they don't loosen. *Courtesy Dan Holiday*

FINISHING SANDALS

To finish sandals trim excess leather from around the sole. Then bevel top and bottom edges. Sand the knife cut marks smooth; seal the edges with burnishing ink (edge enamel) and buff. Apply a generous coating of neat's-foot oil and allow sandals to stand for about ten minutes before buffing. Fit straps snugly for the first few days of wear and then readjust their tension.

SEWING MOCCASINS AND OUTDOOR FOOTWEAR

Moccasins are sewn with thin thonging of rawhide, latigo, or with wax-coated Dacron thread with a cord count of five to eight strands. When sewing moccasins together it is best to use a last, but if a last is not available, stuff it with a plastic sponge or with a plastic bag stuffed full of styrene scraps used in packing. Punch holes, one hole ahead of your needle or needles (if you use a cobbler's stitch), to make certain that holes will line up in the proper progression. You might indicate spacing with marks from a spacing wheel on the smaller vamp section along the edge to assure even spacing. A running stitch or a cross-stitch can be used to attach the heel seam. This seam, by the way, should be up high enough on the heel so as not to get in the way of the downward stroke in walking.

In a moccasin the sole or bottom portion curves upward and traditionally is slightly longer in circumference, requiring some

A WALTER DYER APPROACH TO MAKING A MOCCASIN

Foot last and two moccasin parts are ready. The heel section has been sewn.

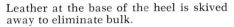

Leather at the base of the heel is skived away to eliminate bulk.

The last is inserted and a few tacks hold parts in place, particularly to mark the center front and center heel (for left and right foot determination).

→

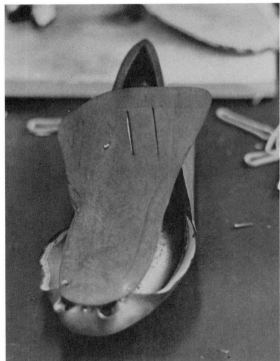

Lasting pliers stretch the leather and tacks are hammered in all around the last to hold the leather in place.

Two kinds of cobbler's stitches are used employing two needles and beeswaxed Dacron thread. After a hole is made for the needles, both needles are strung through the same hole in opposite directions.

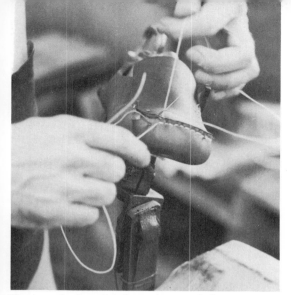

Next, each thread is looped around the point end of each needle (which forms a loop) . . .

. . . and the needles are pulled through the loops.

Another approach is to form a crisscross cobbler stitch. An awl makes a hole, one step ahead of the needles, into the two thicknesses of leather.

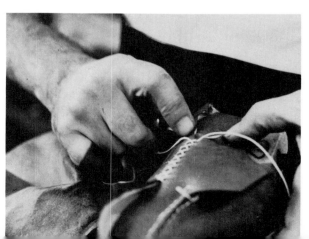

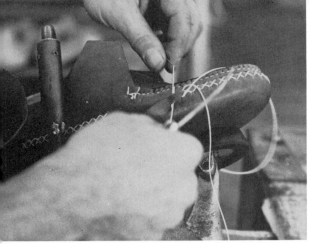

The needles are pushed through the hole, points going in opposite directions.

Thread is crossed over and around the respective needles to form an "x."

And the thread is pulled tautly.

Walter Dyer moccasin-shoes with a decorative cross-stitch treatment. Adjustment for the instep is at the back. *Courtesy Walter Dyer*

Another Walter Dyer moccasin-shoe. *Courtesy Walter Dyer*

A Walter Dyer wraparound boot. A disk of leather is tied through the boot and a thonging loop from the wraparound edge hooks over the leather button to form a unique closing device. *Courtesy Walter Dyer*

gathering and, of course, wider spacing between holes while the vamp is a flat plane. Set your holes back about $3/16$ inch with no more than $3/16$ inch between stitches.

Outdoor boots are made from leather ranging from eight to fourteen ounces. Two wooden lasts are essential because they function as a foundation upon which the leather is formed. They act as a surrogate instep and foot, the same size as the foot that will wear the boot.

The top and upper parts are sewn together. Then the leather is wet and stretched over the instep last. When dry, the back is sewed and fitted. Again the leather is wetted down and folded in half to determine left and

right. It is tacked and stretched over the foot last and allowed to dry before removal. Excess gathering is cut away, leaving a one-inch edge. The inner sole is cut, fitted, and trimmed. Inner and outer soles are glued together sandwiching the boot edge. The wooden last is removed and the boot is placed on a metal last. Clinching nails (extra iron) are used all around the edge to reinforce the bond. Heels are built up layer by layer, and an inner curve is ground.

Excess sole is carved away, sanded, sealed with edge enamel, and buffed.

Bootmaking takes a great deal of skill and certainly graduation from skills of sandal and moccasin making.

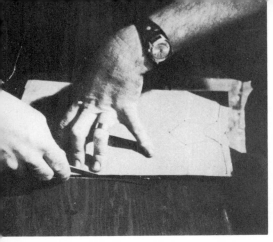

MAKING A BOOT WITH DAN HOLIDAY

A good way for a beginner to attempt the difficult job of bootmaking is to take apart an old boot and use that as a pattern. Dan Holiday uses his own pattern design to cut out the leather parts.

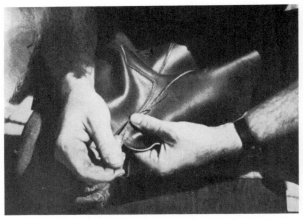

Dan sews the toe and front section of the boot together at the instep by hand stitching, using a waxed linen thread.

He points to a leg last at the curve of the instep. (In the foreground is the waxed linen thread.)

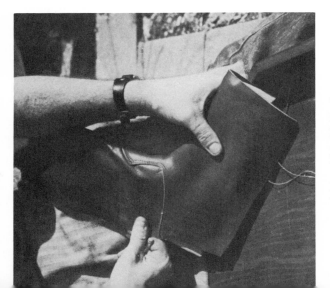

The leather that was just sewn together is soaked in water and then tacked to the last in one or two spots to hold it in place, then stretched and formed over the instep curve. It forms easily. It is kept over the last until it dries. When dry, the back of the boot is sewn (with a good quality waxed linen thread) to form its tube shape. Before trimming and hammering out the seam, the boot is pulled right side out and tried on the leg for any adjustments. Then the boot is turned inside out again and the back seam is trimmed of excess leather and hammered flat.

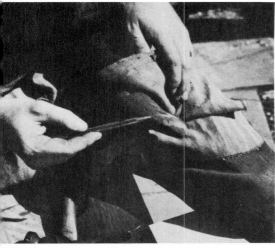

The boot is now placed over a foot last of the correct size (after it has been wet again and folded in half, flat, so that the back center of the heel and front center of the toe has been marked with a pencil). From now on, there is a left and a right boot.

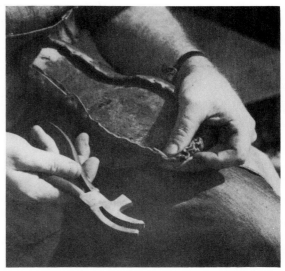

A tack is tacked center heel into center back heel first and then on the center toe to the center front with lasting pliers pulling and tacking. One and a half inches of leather should hang down below the last.

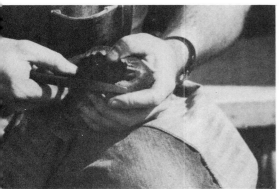

Both sides are worked. After tacking, the boot while on its last is allowed to dry for a day. →

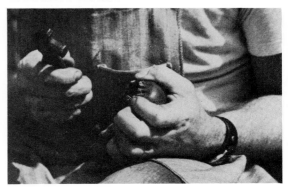

Then tacks are pulled out; the last is removed and excess leather is trimmed to allow for one inch around the edge. An inner sole (eight- or nine-ounce iron) is measured to fit the foot and cut. The last is placed back into the boot and the inner sole inserted, with the one-inch edge overlapping here. Then the inner sole is trimmed, the sole put back behind the boot edge.

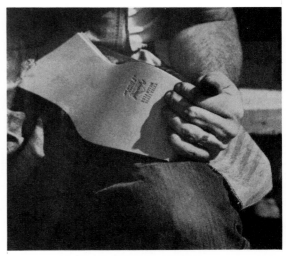

An outer sole (twelve iron and up) is measured, cut, and matched.

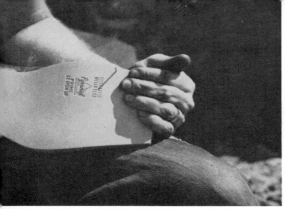

A tack is inserted to hold the outer sole in place.

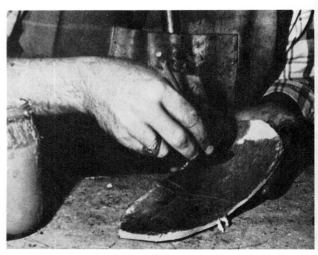

The soles are glued, matched, and pounded together.

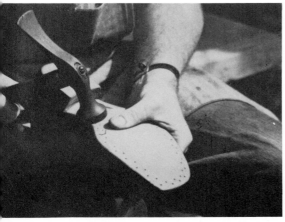

The wooden foot last is pulled out through the throat of the boot (not without difficulty). And the boot is slipped onto a metal bootjack and cobbled with extra iron clinching nails.

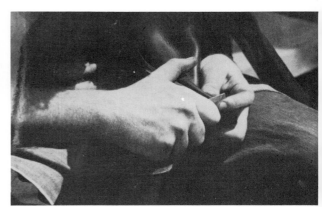

Edges are trimmed and sanded. Heels are glued and stacked, one layer at a time. When built up sufficiently, the inner part of the heel is ground into a curve with a grinding bit.

Dan Holiday displays the completed boot, done in the tradition of the Italian-Austrian-Bavarian method of making a cobbled boot. *Courtesy Dan Holiday*

Another style of boot made with a sewed sole, by Ben Liberty. *Courtesy Ben Liberty.*
Photo by Jeffery Boxer

11

MORE LEATHER
AS AN ART EXPERIENCE

The function and art of leather are integrally related. Some leather forms are useful objects fulfilling a job, others are enjoyed for sensory or aesthetic reasons. Their function often is to communicate nonverbally. Art can be found in both useful and fine art forms. Both have purpose. Useful art, however, is "physically" involved in carrying out a function, such as a pocketbook shape in which to carry sundry items. Fine art has purpose, too. But its existence can be more intangible, more spiritual, and requires the viewer to reach out to it, to bring some experiences and understandings to it, for communication to exist. Certainly this is less concrete than a wallet or briefcase.

Fine art has function and purpose too. "Vase" by Nancy Flanagan.

268

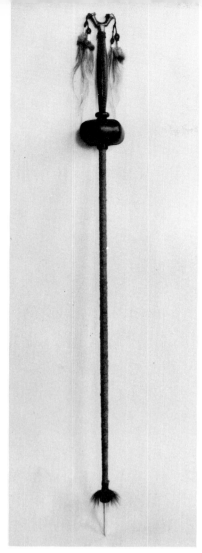

Useful art is "physically" involved in carrying out a function. It depends, though, on how we define "function." "Staff Form" by A. Dean Massey, of leather, metal, and horsehair. *Photo by Jim Fisher; Courtesy A. Dean Massey*

Detail of "Staff Form." *Photo by Jim Fisher*

Fine art can pretend its relationship to function. "Electro-Mechanical Blue Sapphire Laser Projector" by Fred Williams. *Photo by Jim Fisher; Courtesy Fred Williams*

Close-up. Hemispherical projections around left rim were wet formed on the leather. The "lightning symbol" on the body was machine-stitched reverse appliqué. Ends are blow-molded acrylic with acrylic tubing forming the supports, as well as vertical tubing. Something old and something new . . . *Photo by Jim Fisher; Courtesy Fred Williams*

"Leather Ring" by Fred Williams combines leather with a light reflector, golden pheasant tippet features, and brass. *Photo by Jim Fisher; Courtesy Fred Williams*

Sewn and stuffed leather form, with convex mirror and hanging horsehair, by A. Dean Massey. Leather as a skin that evokes a sensual response is played upon by artists. *Courtesy A. Dean Massey*

How well a design or idea is executed is craftsmanship. There is skill in executing a useful design form or a sculpture. Illustrated throughout the book are fine art and functional examples—beautiful and usable forms that fulfill a purpose. Leather in one sense requires involvement through manipulation of the material. And in another sense it communicates an aesthetic appreciation of its attributes—of its surface qualities and pliability. Only when leather is understood for its physical and aesthetic qualities can it be used effectively to execute any kind of form.

Leather is a skin. As a skin it can be textured and colored, cut, stretched, glued, and formed. Through these processes leather can become a surface with enough dimensional stability to contain a volume of air, or it can become a surface covering for another material. Both these concepts are understood and employed by sculptors. Nancy Flanagan wet-forms rawhide into hollow, almost brittle, shell-like volumes that resemble some imaginary sea urchin. Lorne Peterson forms, stretches, sews, and glues different colors and textures of leather into the skin and clothing of his humorous, mechanical creature.

Nancy Flanagan wet-forms rawhide into hollow, almost brittle, shell-like volumes that resemble imaginary sea urchins. "Rawhide Fetish" by Nancy Flanagan. *Courtesy Nancy Flanagan*

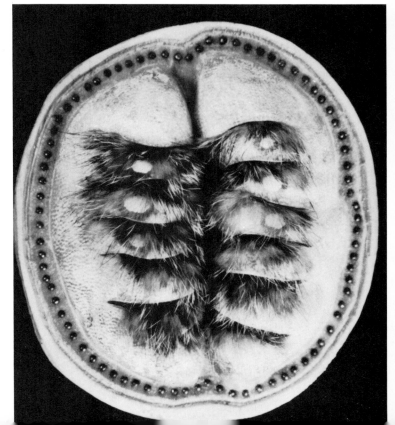

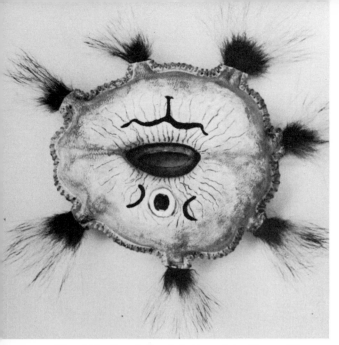

"Rawhide Fetish Rattle" (front) by Nancy Flanagan. *Courtesy Nancy Flanagan*

Back of "Rawhide Fetish Rattle."

"Rawhide Fetish Beads," Nancy Flanagan. *Courtesy Nancy Flanagan*

Lorne Peterson forms, stretches, sews, and glues different colors and textures of leather, fur, and plastic into the skin and clothing of his humorous mechanical creature. And it's a bank, too!

Artists play up the organic qualities of leather by combining it with other organic materials such as wood, fur, and feathers. Often leather accentuates the sensuous aspects of forms through its own sensual qualities. Leather's softness, warmth, pliability, and its special "leather" odor excite the senses.

Artists use leather because of the range of its expressive potential, because it is, above all, malleable. Even when stretched taut and thin as sinew, leather expresses idiomatically the feeling of reaching limits and surviving tests of its endurance. There must be some subliminal feelings about leather, too, because it is a skin and we are covered with skin. The translation from self to the leather form is easy to effect. Nancy Grossman achieves her impact by covering carved wooden heads in a constricture of leather, which is further emphasized with straps and metallic hardware.

Nancy Grossman achieves impact here in "GLS" by covering carved wooden heads in a constricture of leather, which is further emphasized with straps and metallic hardware. *Courtesy Cordier & Ekstrom, Inc.*

More heads by Nancy Grossman. *Courtesy Cordier & Ekstrom, Inc.*

Just as Queen Dido overcame the limitations of the size of a hide to establish the boundaries for her Carthage, so have contemporary sculptors found solutions when expansive size is a requirement. Some artists build large three-dimensional forms by sewing parts together; other laminate and nail smaller units into large forms. Mary Fish, for example, sews, stuffs, and ties leather into a long tubelike sculpture. Leather also can cover an armature or framework with no problems as to size if various colors and textures are combined into larger units as in John Fargotstein's "American Effigy '1971.'"

Mary Fish sews, stuffs, and ties leather into a long tubelike sculpture terminating with fingers. Leather is used here like a skin, like a newspaper, like a snake—yet in an entirely new imagery. *Courtesy Mary Fish*

Leather also can cover an armature or framework with no problem as to size. "American Effigy '1971'" by John Fargotstein. *Courtesy John Fargotstein*

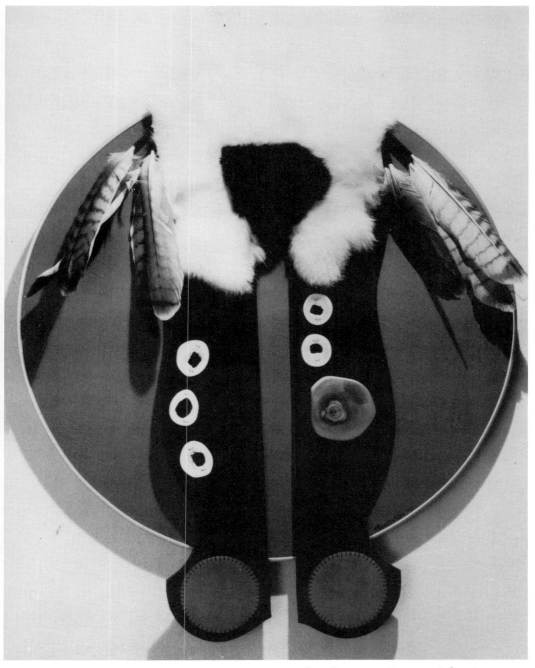

"Shield Form '1972'" by John Fargotstein, 24 inches diameter. *Courtesy John Fargotstein*

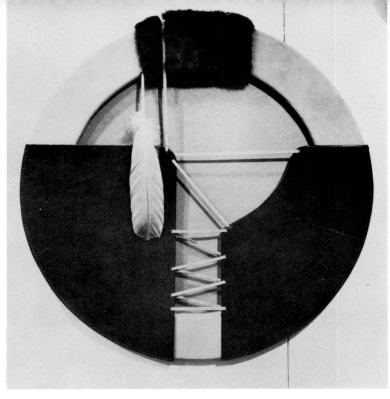

Another shield form by John Fargotstein. *Courtesy John Fargotstein*

Traditionally, the materials of art have been those substances that have withstood the wear and weathering of centuries. Leather has not been one of these materials, because, until recently, it could not compete with stone and metal. But today, with the development of modern tannage practices and surface preservatives for reconditioning leather, an ancient material is becoming a new art medium.

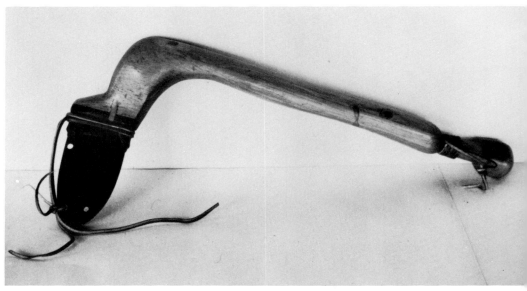

Sculpture of wood and leather by Doug E. Hendrickson. *Courtesy Doug E. Hendrickson*

"Fish" by Doug E. Hendrickson. Wood with leather thong "fins." *Courtesy Doug E. Hendrickson*

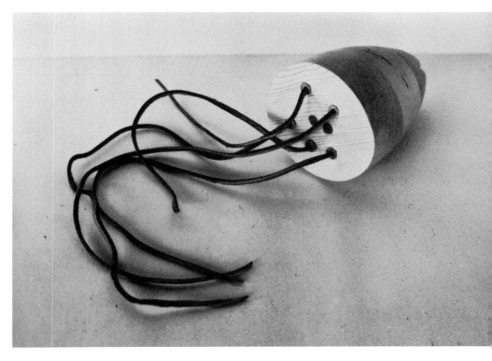

Glossary

Antiquing
A superimposed color streaked and rubbed over a base color.

Appliqué
Attaching one piece of leather over another.

Back
Side with belly cut off.

Bating
Neutralizing of alkalinity after hair removal process.

Belly
Underpart of hide.

Belly center
Middle part of belly with areas cut off.

Belting
Nonstretching leather supplied in round or flat, narrow continuous stripping.

Bends
90 degrees folding.

Bonding agents
Wet or dry glues and cements used to attach parts together.

Braiding
See Plaiting.

Buckskin
Deer or elk skins having the outer grain removed.

Burning
Actually burning or browning of leather with a heated tool, such as an electrically controlled pencil.

Butt end
Unused or remaining portion of hide, such as thigh area.

Cabretta
Hair-type sheepskin.

Calfskin
Skin from a young bovine male or female.

Capeskin

From a sheep raised in South Africa.

Carpincho

A water rodent native to South America, like pigskin.

Carving

Cutting into leather with a knife.

Cased leather

A water-moistened leather. State of leather before tooling.

Chamois

The product of oil tanning the underneath layer, called a "flesher," that has been split from a sheepskin.

Chamoising (oil dressing)

Oils or oil containing materials such as tallow, egg yolks, brains, and liver of cattle, used as a dressing for hides and skins.

Chrome-tanned leather

Leather tanned with minerals such as chromium sulfate or chrome for an open tannage producing a more porous material than vegetable tannage.

Clinching, or cobbler's, nails (Soling nails)

Small metallic blue-gray-black nails with a fine slightly curved point at the end.

Collagen

Cell structure that gives leather its elasticity.

Conditioners

Materials that soften and revitalize non-suede leathers.

Cordovan

Horsehide sumac-tanned and later tanned with an infusion of sumac from a section called the shell.

Corium

Second layer of skin under the epidermis that becomes the basis of leather.

Cowhide

Hide from a mature female bovine that has produced a calf.

Crease

Over 180 degrees when leather folds back on itself.

Crop

Side minus belly portion.

Cross-dyeing

Mixing colors directly on the leather, one color over the other.

Croupon

Most ideal part of the hide, back only, minus shoulder and belly.

Cured hides and skins

Temporary retardation of a protein degradation of hides and skins through use of sodium chloride in wet-salting or use of a brine-curing approach.

Currier's comb

Implement to scrape away hair of hide. Teeth are set in a circle.

Currying

Incorporating oils and grease into leather in order to increase strength, water repellency, and pliability.

Deerskin

Deer and elk skins, having the grain intact.

Doeskin

From sheep or lambskins, usually with the grain removed.

Dubbin

A mixture of cod-liver oil and tallow to dress leather.

Dyes

Usually aniline and come in powder form for mixing with water or alcohol, or mineral oil and spirit solvent.

Embossing (Repoussé)

Stretching leather sections on the back side by rubbing back and forth with a tool to achieve a raised effect on the grain side.

Extreme

A side just larger than a kip, but smaller than cow or steerhides.

Eyelets

Shallow tubes ending up after attachment with rings at both ends.

Fat liquoring

Treatment of leather with soap and oil.

Findings

Miscellaneous parts, usually of metal, used to attach sections or act as closings.

Flesher

Underneath (flesh side) layer of a sheepskin that has been split off. Used to make chamois.

Fleshing (Scuding)

Removal of fatty layer of hides, or skins.

Florentine, or Venetian, lacing

Softer and wider than other laces. Meant to completely cover edges.

Folds

Between 90 and 180 degrees.

Forming

Soaking leather, then stretching and molding it over a wooden form or mold.

Full-grain leathers

Leathers that are not buffed to remove surface scratches, etc.

Glove horse

A supple horsehide used for garments given exposure to weather.

Grommet

A two-piece finding with a collarlike flange on a tube for one section and a separate ring for the other.

Guadamacileros

Spanish leatherworkers who excelled in creating figured leather.

Hair calf

Skin of calf with hair intact. When hair is clipped short it is called *hair calf clipped.*

Harness

Vegetable-tanned cattlehide leather finished for harness, saddlery, sculpture.

Hides

Leather from large animals such as horses, cows, buffalo.

Horsehide

Hide from horse, or colt.

Incising

Cutting away areas of leather usually in thin slivers.

Iron

One iron is equal to a piece that measures $\frac{1}{48}$ inch thick.

Kipskin

Skin from bovine, male or female, intermediate in size between a calf and a mature animal.

Lacing

Usually $\frac{3}{32}$ to $\frac{3}{16}$ inch wide and curved at edges. Often used to attach parts together.

Lamellé

Rare type of embroidery with thin pieces of metal strips.

Laminating

Building height or depth by cementing many thicknesses of leather one over the other.

Latigo

Cowhide sides tanned with alum, gambier (yellowish catechu), and oil. Used for saddle strings, lacing, carved forms, sculpture.

Leather

The hide, or skin, of an animal (usually mammal or reptile) that has been preserved by dressing (tawing or tanning) into a stable, nonputrescible, flexible sheet.

Live oak

Vegetable-tanned cowhide producing a clear and even grain. Good for tooling, sculpture, etc.

Modeling

Depressing areas around outlines so some parts stand out in relief.

Morocco

Goatskin, sumac-tanned and dyed red.

Oil Dressing

See Chamoising.

Oxalic acid

With water, used to clean leather surface before dyeing.

Parchment

Made from the split skins of sheep exposed for a long time to lime, then scraped with a rounded knife or rubbed smooth with pumice stone. Not a true leather.

Patchwork

Juxtaposing one piece of leather next to another and attaching them side by side.

Pelt

An untanned hide, or skin, with hair left on.

Pickling

Placement of skins in a low pH environment in chrome tanning for skins to accept tanning agents.

Plaiting (Braiding)

Use of interwoven strips of leather to make linear objects such as straps, belts, etc.

Plating

Ironing, or pressing, operation that introduces another surface texture to leather.

Raw stock

General term for hides, or skins, that a tanner has received in a preserved state, preparatory to tanning.

Repoussé

See Embossing.

Rivets

Permanent fasteners used to attach parts and to add decoration.

Russian leather

Calfskin dressed with birch oil.

Saddle skirting

Very heavy cowhide sides vegetable-tanned for saddles. Good for sculpture too.

Scuding

See Fleshing.

Side

One half of a skin, or hide.

Single bend

One half of the section of the back of a hide.

Skins

Leather from small animals such as calves, kids, etc.

Skiver

The thin grain layer split from a sheepskin.

Skiving

Thinning of leather edges and areas usually with a knife or special skiving tool to remove excess leather.

Slunk

Skin of unborn or prematurely born calf, tanned with hair left intact.

Split

Layer of hide from under the top grain.

Staking

Mechanically flexing, pulling, and rolling skins and hides to achieve different degrees of softness.

Stamping

Use of metal dyes to press out a design.

Steerhide

Hide from a mature male bovine, incapable of reproduction, having been raised for beef.

Suede

Leather-finishing process whereby the flesh side on top of a split is buffed to produce a nap.

Sweating

Removal of hair from hide by placing it in urine to increase alkalinity and hasten decay of hair.

Tannin

Tanning ingredients found in a variety of sources, usually trees and shrubs.

Tanning

Irreversible process of introducing tanning materials (tannins) into leather to form a chemical bond and thereby preserve the hide, or skin.

Tawing

Salt and alum dressing used as temporary preservatives for hides and skins. Process is reversible because neither salt nor alum is absorbed chemically into the hide.

Tempering

Controlling the softness of leather.

Thonging

Narrow strip of leather used usually to attach parts.

Tooling

An overall term encompassing the mechanical manipulation of leather to create permanent depressions and raised areas of design.

Vegetable-tanned leather

Oak and other vegetable stuffs used as the essential ingredient in the tanning process.

Vellum

Made from calfskin, goatskin, or lambskin, exposed for a long time to lime, and then scraped with a rounded knife or rubbed smooth with pumice stone. Not a true leather.

Venetian lacing

See Florentine.

Bibliography

CHERRY, RAYMOND. *General Leathercraft.* Bloomington, Illinois: McKnight & McKnight Publishing Co., 1955.

GRANT, BRUCE. *Leather Braiding.* Cambridge, Maryland: Cornell Maritime Press, Inc., 1961.

GRISWOLD, KATHLEEN AND LESTER. *The New Handicraft.* New York: Van Nostrand Reinhold Co., 1972.

HODGES, HENRY. *Artifacts.* London: John Baker, 1971.

HUNT, BEN. *Big Indiancraft Book.* New York: The Bruce Publishing Co., 1945.

KREVITSKY, NIK. *Batik Art and Craft.* New York: Reinhold Publishing Co., 1964.

Leather Facts. Peabody, Massachusetts: New England Tanners' Club, 1972.

Leather in Our Lives. New York: Leather Industries of America. n.d.

MEILACH, DONA Z. *Contemporary Leather.* Chicago: Henry Regnery Co., 1971.

MOSLEY, SPENCER; JOHNSON, PAULINE; AND KOENIG, HAZEL. *Crafts Design.* Belmont, California: Wadsworth Publishing Co., Inc., 1963.

PARKER, XENIA LEY. *Working with Leather.* New York: Charles Scribner's Sons, 1972.

SALMON, JULIAN HARRIS. *The Book of Indian Crafts and Indian Lore.* New York: Harper & Row, Publishers, 1928.

SCHWEBKE, PHYLLIS W., AND KROHN, MARGARET B. *How to Sew Leather, Suede, Fur.* New York: The Bruce Publishing Co., 1970.

SNYDER, W. E. *The Leathercraftsman.* Worcester, Massachusetts: Copyright Acquired American Handicrafts, 1939.

STOHLMAN, AL. *How to Color Leather.* Copyright "The Leather Craftsman" Craftool Co., 1961.

WILLCOX, DONALD. *Modern Leather Design.* New York: Watson-Guptill Publications, 1969.

WULFF, HANS E. *The Traditional Crafts of Persia.* Cambridge, Massachusetts: The M.I.T. Press, 1966.

Sources of Supplies

Adhesives

Allied Shoe Machinery Cement Corp.
    241 Winter Street
    Haverhill, Massachusetts 01830

Barge Cement Division
National Starch & Chemical Corp.
    100 Jacksonville Road
    Towaco, New Jersey 07082

Craftsman All-Purpose Cement
    At all Tandy Leather Company Stores

Elmer's Glue
Borden Chemical Co.
    350 Madison Avenue
    New York, New York 10017

Epoxy
Devcon Corporation
    Endicott Street
    Danvers, Massachusetts 01923

Goodyear High Speed Neolite All-Purpose
    Cement
Goodyear Rubber Co.
    132 Duane Street
    New York, New York 10013

Petronio Glue
Petronio Shoe Products
    1447 McCarter Highway
    Newark, New Jersey 07100

Plasti-Tak
Brooks Manufacturing Co.
    1051 Meredith Drive
    Cincinnati, Ohio 45231

Sanford's Elephant Glue
   Bellwood, Illinois 60104

Sobo, Quik
Slomon's Labs, Inc.
   32–45 Hunter's Point Ave.
   Long Island City, New York 11101

Weldwood Contact Cement
U.S. Plywood Corp.
   2305 Superior Street
   Kalamazoo, Michigan 49003

Cork

Bradley Enterprises
   Main Street
   Bradley Beach, New Jersey 07720

Dodge Cork Co.
   Lancaster, Pennsylvania 17604

Dies

John J. Adams Die Corp.
   P.O. Box 157
   Worcester, Massachusetts 01613

Auburn Die Co.
   Auburn, Maine 04103

Boston Cutting Die Company
   50 Freeport Street
   Boston, Massachusetts 02122

Chicago Cutting Die Co.
   2325 Nelson Street
   Chicago, Illinois 60618

C. S. Osborne & Co.
   125 Jersey Street
   Harrison, New Jersey 07029

United Shoe Machinery Corp.
   140 Federal Street
   Boston, Massachusetts 02110

Dyes for Coloring

Fezan Colors
Fezandie & Sperrie, Inc.
   103 Lafayette Street
   New York, New York 10013

Fibrec
   2795 16th Street
   San Francisco, California 94103

Fiebling Chemical Co.
   516 2nd Street
   Milwaukee, Wisconsin 53202

D. D. Holiday & Co.
   15 St. George Street
   St. Augustine, Florida 32084

John Lincoln Co.
   Sunnyvale, California 94036

Master Chemical Co.
   27 Brandston Street
   Boston, Massachusetts 02100

Omega Leathercraft Products Co.
   Fort Worth, Texas 76100
   Los Angeles, California 90052

Hazel Pearson
   4128 Temple City Boulevard
   Rosemead, California 91770

Rit Dyes
Best Food Co.
   Indianapolis, Indiana 46206

Tisfine Ink (Edge Coatings)
United Shoe Machinery Chemical Co.
   Middleton, Massachusetts 01949

Findings

All Kind of Metal Ornamentation
American Shoe Specialties Co., Inc.
   318 West 39th Street
   New York, New York 10018

Brass Nails, Rivets, Buckles
Berman Leather Co.
   147 South Street
   Boston, Massachusetts 02111

Buckles and all Kinds of Attachments
North & Judd
A Gulf & Western Co.
   P.O. Box 1111
   Middletown, Connecticut 06457

Buckles and Ornamentation
Stan Levin Metal Products Corp.
   236 West 26th Street
   New York, New York 10001

Buckles—Brass and Pewter
Star Buckle Co., Inc.
   Box 215
   Spinnerstown, Pennsylvania 18968